A VERY SHORT, FAIRLY INTERESTING AND REASONABLY CHEAP BOOK ABOUT

ENTREPRENEURSHIP

A VERY SHORT,
FAIRLY INTERESTING AND
REASONABLY CHEAP BOOK ABOUT

ENTREPRENEURSHIP

MIKE ZUNDEL AND
CHRISTIAN G. JOHNSEN

S Sage

S Sage

1 Oliver's Yard
55 City Road
London EC1Y 1SP

2455 Teller Road
Thousand Oaks
California 91320

Unit No 323-333, Third Floor, F-Block
International Trade Tower, Nehru Place
New Delhi 110 019

8 Marina View Suite 43-053
Asia Square Tower 1
Singapore 018960

**Library of Congress Control Number:
2024945396**

British Library Cataloguing in Publication data

A catalogue record for this book is available from
the British Library

Editor: Emma Yuan
Editorial assistant: Clara Landgren
Production editor: Rabia Barkatulla
Copyeditor: Raxshana Ravindraraj
Proofreader: Girish Sharma
Marketing manager: Elena Asplen
Cover design: Bhairvi Vyas
Typeset by: TNQ Tech Pvt. Ltd.
Printed in the UK

ISBN 978-1-5296-8007-2
ISBN 978-1-5296-8006-5 (pbk)

[ALSO IN THIS SERIES]

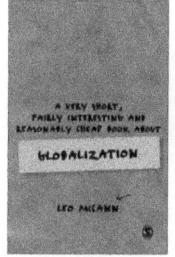

A VERY SHORT, FAIRLY INTERESTING AND REASONABLY CHEAP BOOK ABOUT
GLOBALIZATION

LEO McCANN

SECOND EDITION

A VERY SHORT, FAIRLY INTERESTING AND REASONABLY CHEAP BOOK ABOUT
INTERNATIONAL BUSINESS

GEORGE CAIRNS AND MARTYNA SLIWA

A VERY SHORT, FAIRLY INTERESTING AND REASONABLY CHEAP BOOK ABOUT
EMPLOYMENT RELATIONS

TONY DUNDON, NIALL CULLINANE AND ADRIAN WILKINSON

A VERY SHORT, FAIRLY INTERESTING AND REASONABLY CHEAP BOOK ABOUT
Human Resource Management

IRENA GRUGULIS

FOURTH EDITION

A VERY SHORT, FAIRLY INTERESTING AND REASONABLY CHEAP BOOK ABOUT
STUDYING ORGANIZATIONS

CHRIS GREY

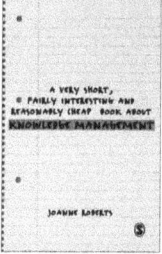

A VERY SHORT, FAIRLY INTERESTING AND REASONABLY CHEAP BOOK ABOUT
KNOWLEDGE MANAGEMENT

JOANNE ROBERTS

A VERY SHORT, FAIRLY INTERESTING AND REASONABLY CHEAP BOOK ABOUT
INTERNATIONAL MARKETING

AMANDA EARLEY

A VERY SHORT, FAIRLY INTERESTING AND REASONABLY CHEAP BOOK ABOUT
MANAGEMENT RESEARCH

EMMA BELL AND RICHARD THORPE

A VERY SHORT, FAIRLY INTERESTING AND REASONABLY CHEAP BOOK ABOUT
QUALITATIVE RESEARCH

SECOND EDITION

DAVID SILVERMAN

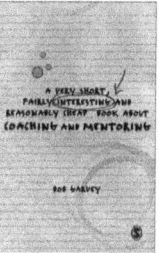

A VERY SHORT, FAIRLY INTERESTING AND REASONABLY CHEAP BOOK ABOUT
COACHING AND MENTORING

BOB GARVEY

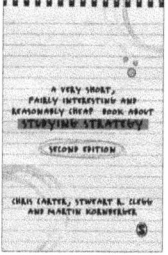

A VERY SHORT, FAIRLY INTERESTING AND REASONABLY CHEAP BOOK ABOUT
STUDYING STRATEGY

SECOND EDITION

CHRIS CARTER, STEWART R. CLEGG AND MARTIN KORNBERGER

A VERY SHORT, FAIRLY INTERESTING AND REASONABLY CHEAP BOOK ABOUT
MANAGEMENT THEORY

TODD BRIDGMAN STEPHEN CUMMINGS

Contents

Contents

About the Authors

Mike Zundel is a Professor of Organisation Studies at the University of Liverpool Management School. He is interested in processual and ecological approaches to strategy, entrepreneurship and organisation theory, with a particular interest in cybernetics and media theory. With Robin Holt, he recently published a monograph, *The Poverty of Strategy*, investigating the influence of technology on organisation and the possibility of an open and authentic way of being.

Christian Garmann Johnsen is an Associate Professor at the Department of Business Humanities and Law at Copenhagen Business School. His research interests lie in the intersection of organisation studies, entrepreneurship research, business ethics and philosophy. These interests have led him to develop different research projects, including a study of sustainable entrepreneurship, authentic leadership and management innovation.

Introduction

new pots

In his marvellous book *Playing to the Gallery* (2015), Grayson Perry reflects on how he, an outsider artist, ended up in the centre of the art industry. Perry is most famous for ceramics which he crafts in small numbers in a simple workshop in London, and which sell for substantial amounts of money. He has also gained public and critical recognition, being the recipient of the prestigious Turner and Erasmus art prizes and a knighthood in 2023. Perry provides an intriguing starting point for our discussion of entrepreneurship, a label we often attribute to people who create new product genres and entice new customer audiences. Perry fits the bill: his work helped change the perception of pottery, which was hitherto seen to be more domestic or ornamental than 'fine arts'. Yet, he is not only an artistic entrepreneur (Hjorth and Holt, 2016) but also an enterprising one. His artworks are widely popular, and he has become a prominent figure in news and media, attracting new audiences to galleries and attracting more people to join the business of art, making, buying, or enjoying not just ceramics, but also tapestries, fashion, writing, and much more.

Reading up to understand how Perry 'did it', we quickly happen upon some good stories. One stretches back to school days where, having been 'naughty', he was put in a girls' pottery class. There he fell in love with clay and with the erotic frill of being helped into a protective PVC smock that was a bit too tight and a bit too shiny and blue, by a teaching assistant who was a bit too pretty. As origin stories go, this is pretty good fare, and we may put Perry down as a flamboyant, clever, creative, and immensely eloquent person whose self-reliant, confident, and risk-taking personality allows him to spot, seize, and exploit the opportunity to turn pottery into high art. Such a 'right character meets golden opportunity' story implies that some people are equipped with specific entrepreneurial genes, or that they have acquired the right kinds of attitudes and skills to be entrepreneurially successful. This suggests that opportunities exist out there, waiting to be discovered by entrepreneurially-minded people who spot a good deal before others who are left jumping onto the bandwagon.

Another story we could tell is about experimenting, as Perry did, with a range of things, such as performance art, making films and pottery, and then with styles, materials, messages and so on, before sticking to what turned out to be working. Rather than waiting for the right opportunity to come along, experimental entrepreneurs have a few projects on the go, and they test them to see what happens. The difference between the opportunity discovery and experimental approaches is that the former is often a one-off shot at an opportunity (before others spot it), while the latter unfolds in iterative steps, where entrepreneurs listen to feedback from their customers, competitors and investors, and then drop what does not work, or tinker and adjust things as they go along.

Yet another story might begin with Perry's working-class upbringing in which the prospects of a 'career' in art, and then of actually making a living, were vanishingly small (Perry, 2015: 128). In this context, the art world presents a hostile, nepotistic, and elitist cabal, guarded by art dealers whose own reputations legitimise an artist's output. And in the 1980s art scene of 'big London' (Jones, 2006: 141), the idea of an artist potter (or more specifically, 'an Essex transvestite potter', Perry, 2015: 2) did not signal the right background or artistic provenance, nor was it just sufficiently rebellious enough to be on the verge of consumer acceptance (Perry, 2015: 80). There is a disarming charm in Perry's self-depreciatively humourous telling of how he came to 'make it', which only thinly veils its vulnerabilities. We read of persistence in face of failure, coincidences, but perhaps most of all, a love for doing what you do. It is almost a complete counterimage of the self-reliant and utterly capable entrepreneur who happens to possess the right personality traits. In Perry's account we feel that it is precisely the insecurities, the not being settled or clear about what or who one is that amount to a sense of un-at-homeness in the world. And it is this uncanny condition that can spark something quite extraordinarily creative.

Perry's account sets us into a direction to think entrepreneurship not based on knowing things in advance, perhaps not even knowing anything for certain at all, or even finding solutions to clear-cut problems, but a playfully searching way of giving expression to things that are not yet in the world. It points to a way of understanding entrepreneurship associated with birthing matters we have not yet necessarily thought about and the disclosure of concepts and ideas for which we have not yet coined the right words, created rules, stories, histories, or routines, or for which we have no affective repertoires and therefore can't quite attach a value.

Our likening of entrepreneurship to an artistic process is deliberate, emphasising a transformative creative (and creat-*ing*) character that brings about something new. This makes entrepreneurship a messy affair that exceeds more straightforward ideas that connect person-ality traits with spotting gaps in a market. It also broadens entrepre-neurship from purely economic 'enterprising' activity to include a wide range of reflexive engagements that harbour the potential to transform both the entrepreneurial environment and the entrepreneurs themselves. A big part of such entrepreneurial artistry has to do with creating sensibilities, language, familiarity, and acceptance of and for new things in a world that is already busily engaged in dealing with established and settled affairs. It entails telling stories, drawing images or acting out new ways of thinking, doing, and talking, often playfully or experimentally, so that something new can leave first faint foot-prints that may gradually widen into well-trodden paths. Here we may object, as Perry has stuck to his small and craft-based operation rather than build or 'scale' this into a large business empire. But perhaps that, too, depends on perspective, because in touching and motivating many others beyond the strict confines of a single workshop, does it not thereby become part of a change in the wider world of which it is a part?

who may be interested in this book and why

This, more or less, is the account of entrepreneurship we want to develop in this book. We take inspiration from some extraordinary contributions to the academic literature on entrepreneurship and organisation studies, to which we hope this book serves as an invitation and introduction. We also take licence from the quirkily titled 'VSFIRC' book format to try and do what Joan Didion (2021) calls 'talking directly to the reader', that is, neither attempting to inform nor writing responsibly and seri-ously from objective distance. For Didion, this means assuming that the reader is a friend with a shared language and a common ethic who may be concerned about something and therefore understanding of the straight talking. In this, we try to follow the footsteps of the VSFIRC, and especially Chris Grey's (2005) inaugural contribution, to develop a take on the theme of entrepreneurship from our own point of view. We find entrepreneurship exciting, both in terms of the ways in which ventures are created, sustained, grow and change and in terms of the academic writings that try to make sense of such activity in the context of wider social, economic, ecological, and, increasingly, technological affairs. What also intrigues us is that despite the attention entrepre-neurship has received from academics, it still feels like an open and exciting topic attracting contributors and readers who remain empiri-cally and intellectually curious.

Empirically, entrepreneurship concerns many different ways of life. It is a central policy tool when it comes to creating jobs and fostering equality; it is seen to be key in alleviating poverty and regenerating deprived regions. Social entrepreneurship manages to do good while also making money or, at least, funding itself, and so replaces alternative ways of addressing social and natural imbalances, thereby shifting responsibilities. No longer just associated with starting businesses, we find administrative, social, and employment practices infused by entrepreneurial idea(l)s: Cities, councils, and public health providers are encouraged to act entrepreneurially by competing, demonstrating value for money and taking risks. Institutions providing social care services, including charities, act entrepreneurially when they come up with cost-saving initiatives or when they invest in new ventures. Meanwhile, universities have become entrepreneurial not just in terms of commercialising their research but also by way of international expansion, investing in conference centres or student accommodation, and driving continuous pedagogical innovation, often based on new communication technologies. Entrepreneurship even stretches to career plans as such, as it is no longer enough to learn a profession or gain skill sets that set one up for a lifetime of work. Rather than expecting life-long employment, workers have to update themselves so that even large and bureaucratic organisations can benefit from the 'intrapreneurial' zeal that is released when their employees act autonomously and proactively, when they innovate and exhibit competitive aggressiveness and take risks to potentially win or lose something from their actions. Such an 'entrepreneurial orientation' is now routinely developed in graduate programmes teaching students how to be creative, preparing them for a workplace where they are required to exceed rather than merely meet expectations. This book may be of interest to those seeking to understand why it is now everyone's own responsibility to upgrade skills, or, better, re-invent oneself entirely, not just to keep up with the changing demands of the workplace but also to be the originators of constant change. Standing still means falling behind.

We explore these trends via the notion of the 'entrepreneurial society' to reflect on the encroachment of innovation and risk-taking and, in particular, the drive for continuous creativity, by which expectations and responsibilities shift from social groups to individuals. We also explore how recent technological advances coupled with greater freedom allow many more groups in society to start their own business, rather than 'just' selling their labour. It has never been easier to become an entrepreneur when all you need to do is download an app to pick up rides delivering food or renting out our apartments or sofas. Examining this interplay of technology and entrepreneurship may be of interest to those involved in policy-making, which often places enterprising activity at the heart of regeneration and development efforts, often modelling expectations on the growth and success of the Silicon Valley.

Intellectually, entrepreneurship is grounded in the notion of disruption unleashing the creative potential that lies dormant when things are stable and static. This places a premium on ground-breaking technological developments that spawn products and services capable of breaking up existing practices, and so create outsized market shares and profits for a small number of startups. But do the positive effects of disruption always justify the disbandment of practices, regulations, or infrastructure, and does it necessarily legitimise the pain, suffering, and hardship for those whose lives are disrupted? And what about those entrepreneurs hoping to find the right combination of factors that attracts investors, while working countless hours in aggressive conditions surrounded by the continuous threat of failure or breakdown?

Tech-based disruptive ventures that manage to scale quickly generate the image of successful entrepreneurs on social media, in the popular – as well as serious – press, as well as on airport bookshelves. This in turn fuels the political mantra of creating high-tech clusters and influences business schools to offer entrepreneurship courses that emulate game-show-style formats where investors pick promising ventures from a long line of people more or less desperately trying to flog their ideas to the highest bidder. Unpacking such ideas and questioning their suitability may be of interest for those studying or teaching entrepreneurship courses, and more broadly to those seeking to set out on their journey with the image of the ultra-successful disrupter in mind, or who want to explore more broadly how to think about starting a venture. In our own experiences of teaching entrepreneurship courses, for example, we see only few students now who come up with business ideas that are not 'apps' or who begin by considering what it may be like, day-to-day, to work towards forming and growing an organisation: the bureaucratic challenges of starting up, logistics, financing, dealing with regulations and so on. Moreover, we continually see students getting stuck when they come up with a business idea and realise after a quick internet search that someone else has already thought of it or quickly such ideas may be copied or emulated by larger and better-resourced companies. Perhaps it is not enough to teach students how to tell the right stories, including those of rapid scaling, filling in business model forms, running through simulations or preparing them to deliver investor 'pitches' as if this was the endpoint of the entrepreneurial journey and more needs to be said about how to deal with everyday or long-term issues, let alone what it may mean to do things because one likes to do them or because they feel like the right things to do.

This book may also be of interest to those intrigued by the more sinister underbelly of the digital technologies and the biosciences associated with – but by no means confined to – the entrepreneurial ventures of the 'Silicon Valley'. There is an increasing dependency of us all, including large institutions and nation-states, on the technological fixes provided by entrepreneurial ventures: they provide tools for communication, banking, entertainment, and shopping; they enable us all to start up a business cheaply, provide ways to advertise, facilitate sales and payment, utilise geo-tracking and navigation and so on; in short, they provide all the kit that makes it possible for us to live and work in contemporary society. They also step in when governments need vaccines or satellite communication systems or when politicians need to win elections. We consider the balance by which everyone can easily own or access means of production through cheap or free apps, programmes or online services, and so be their own boss, but doing so by giving up information about themselves that is harvested, computed, and sold on for advertising and other purposes. We also consider how especially the digital technology industry is not just a neutral provider of tools and infrastructure, but how its very entrepreneurial ethos is wrapped up in politics whose aims and imaginaries are not necessarily always obvious or benign. This may be of interest to those intrigued by the ways in which institutional powers have shifted from nation-states to large corporations and then to startups, as well as from real flesh-and-blood people to the dynamics and algorithms of platforms and networked computing systems. These discussions may also be of interest to those who, like us, wonder if everything, from public services to private time, one's car or home, can or should be seen through the prism of entrepreneurship. At the same time, we acknowledge that advanced technology is part of our environment and that entrepreneurship will play an important role in establishing which of its possibilities are realised and how these changes will come to affect our lives.

While much attention on social media and in the news, as well as by many policy-makers, is placed on (technology-driven) disruption, we find that there is much more to entrepreneurship. The majority of entrepreneurial ventures are not glitz and glam scale and get rich outfits, but operate at a more mundane and less noticed level and yet, owing to the sheer scale of such 'everyday' forms of entrepreneurship, collectively they do a lot of heavy lifting. The final section of the book returns to this connection between entrepreneurship and everyday ways of living and working, and it asks how we may think of creativity and experimentation beyond (or perhaps, rather, below) business model and lean approaches, but also without requiring or expecting a disruption of the old. This book may therefore also be of interest to those who, like us, try to figure out appropriate theories of/for entrepreneurship rather than assuming that the topic is either too diverse or too trivially concerned with creating something new that it is simply atheoretical (something indicated by the many shelves in airport bookstores stacked with colourful biographies, how-to books or anecdotal stories purveyed by 'successful' entrepreneurs) or even anti-theoretical (theory deriving from patterns of the old, which the new has to overcome).

We take inspiration from a tradition in philosophy called 'phenomenology'. There are many differences and deviations in what may be meant by this awkward term. It combines *phenomeno* – which indicates 'light', 'appearance' or 'that which comes to light' – and *logic* – meaning 'word', 'language', or 'the study of'. So, we are dealing with attempts at expressing how things appear – to perception. There is a certain and unavoidable circularity here that defies our sense of scientific objectivity and logical linearity. Things appear not in the abstract, but in the context of perception, which shapes and is shaped by what appears. A landscape, for example, is not one thing that looks more accurate in bright sunlight and more washed out on a misty or rainy da, where it lacks detail and colour. Each appearance is instead singularly valid on its own terms. A landscape presents itself to perception differently – it is different – on different days and if the perceiver is in a good or bad mood, and so the scope for appearance is endless and open, as all elements in play: landscape, perceiver, and the process of perception are all in continuous flux. This brings a new sense of theory: not as a way of reducing complexity, averaging out differences, and conserving what persists, but as a way of accounting for the inherent plurality and burgeoning difference in which the world appears.

Phenomenology is therefore an intriguing mode of thinking in which entrepreneurship, novelty, and creativity may be located in their own terms – not as being atheoretical or against theory, but as an exemplification of a phenomenological way of letting things appear differently. This is also quite different from economics, where, as we will see, many business school approaches to entrepreneurship begin, and from psychology, another big influence when it comes to looking for entrepreneurial characteristics in a person's behavioural or cognitive traits. Phenomenological thinking leads us to suggest that entrepreneurial creativity does not necessarily require an extraordinary event accomplished by the genius discoverer or innovator. Nor are there opportunities out there, lying in waiting for foresightful founders or enterprising risk-takers to happen upon them. Instead, the new is around us all the time, like Perry's earthenware pots, which required a new way of looking to become pieces of art. If we see the world appearing continually in refreshing, surprising, and wonderous ways, then all we need to do is forget the conceptual apparatuses, theories, and taxonomies that continually and automatically tell us in advance what things are. We need, in other words, new eyes to look at the world afresh. This book attempts to introduce a few basic ideas, and point to relevant readings, about such new eyes.

1

Entrepreneurship as Economic Activity

balancing acts

An immensely well-cited journal article by Scott Shane and Sankaran Venkataraman (2000) drives a big definitional stake into the field of entrepreneurship. It suggests that the two moving parts of entrepreneurship are enterprising individuals and the presence of opportunities. These parts are connected by what the authors call a 'nexus'. Conceiving entrepreneurship in terms of such a two-body problem yields research questions along the lines of why opportunities exist, how can opportunities be sized, and what characteristics individuals possess to spot and exploit them. For Shane and Venkataraman, opportunities designate 'those situations in which new goods, services, raw materials, and organizing methods can be introduced and sold at greater than their cost of production' (2000: 220). Such thinking has a long historical tail, harking back in particular to the work of Israel Kirzner (1997), a student of the Austrian school of economics, which emphasises the dynamic nature of the market process that is driven by the actions of the entrepreneur, a figure who in Kirzner's (1997) words, is 'alert' to price discrepancies that yield opportunities for pure profits (Lilley & Lightfoot, 2014):

> Except in the never-attained state of complete equilibrium, each market is characterized by opportunities for pure entrepreneurial profit. These opportunities are created by earlier entrepreneurial errors which have resulted in shortages, surplus, misallocated resources. The daring, alert entrepreneur discovers these earlier errors, buys where prices are "too low" and sells where prices are "too high." In this way low prices are nudged higher, high prices are nudged lower; price discrepancies are narrowed in the equilibrative direction. Shortages are filled, surpluses are whittled away; quantity gaps tend to be eliminated in the equilibrative direction. (Kirzner, 1997: 70)

Opportunities arise when supply and demand for products or services are not coordinated, that is when markets are not (as is often assumed) in natural states of equilibrium. Being out of kilter, the market needs a little help, and it is the entrepreneurial figure of action (rather than a regulator such as the state) who rises to the challenge, discovering opportunities when they come along. In Kirzner's (1997: 70) view, entrepreneurs are alert to opportunities by discovering market errors, such as product or service shortages, and exploit these by acquiring resources at lower prices than they can later sell them for. Thus, 'the entrepreneur is at all times scanning the horizon, as it were, ready to make discoveries' (Kirzner, 1997: 72). By taking advantage of price discrepancies, entrepreneurs help move the market towards equilibrium by serving unmet needs and correcting resource misallocations. One interesting aspect here is that the entrepreneur does not need to possess the means of production, they only need to recognise and act on opportunities profiting from unexploited gain ('arbitrage'), which means they are not just rational calculators but also risk-takers, which in turn justifies their profits (Plehwe, 2020).

We can now see why Shane and Venkataraman (2000) focus on the individual plus opportunity. Entrepreneurs identify, evaluate, and exploit opportunities by introducing new market offerings, thereby remedying (the inter-temporal disequilibrium of) market imperfections. Not only does the opportunity-entrepreneur couplet help explain something about markets, but it also seems to provide the two minimum and foundational criteria for an academic field of entrepreneurship studies.

But as it always is with simple and clear things, they quickly become messy when they meet reality. For example, we may ask *when* an opportunity can be identified. For Kirzner, an opportunity arises when an entrepreneur can '"see" future prices more correctly than others see them' (2009: 148). But, of course, an entrepreneur can at best hazard a guess about the future, because only after a market offering has been launched does the price actually come into being. Now, if that price is higher than the associated costs, then an opportunity exists; if it is lower or if consumers reject the market offering, then no opportunity was present in the first place. But if the existence of an opportunity can only be established after the entrepreneur has acted, then a lot of the definitional tidiness brought by Shane and Venkataraman's contribution starts to look decidedly messy (Dimov, 2011). Part of the problem is that Kirzner (2009) never laid claim to theorise the nature of entrepreneurship. His objective was to understand the market process, and the balancing acts performed by entrepreneurs, at a much higher, economic level.

Then there is the idea of the alert person of action. Shane and Venkataraman's (2000) appropriation of the economic function of the entrepreneur takes place against the backdrop of previous attempts to map entrepreneurial personality characteristics and psychological profiles. This line of research produced various hypotheses, such as the assumption that entrepreneurs differ from other individuals by virtue of higher propensities for risk-taking, more extroversion or fewer existential worries, or they see entrepreneurs being equipped with superior organising skills, cross-cultural experiences, drive, sense of self, resilience, discipline, resourcefulness, and so on. There has been a lot of pushback against these ideas. Especially the work of Bill Gartner (1988) warned against creating a caricature of a superhuman being whose behavioural and personality features make them outperform, outrisk, outsmart and outachieve what mere mortals can cobble together (Drakopoulou Dodd & Anderson, 2007; Sørensen, 2008). Gartner (1988) instead suggests we should focus on the actual work that goes into entrepreneurs creating organisations.

An example is Terry Allen's (2007) own reflections on being involved in starting a toy store in 1965. In this story, we find a bunch of entrepreneurs who spot this opportunity as a combination of favourable factors: a town where no toys are sold outside of Christmas; only one, somewhat lethargic competitor; an empty retail outlet; an interested bank manager; and so on. They realise and exploit this opportunity by being risk-taking, resourceful, at times a bit deviant (evading the bank manager), tenacious, clever (when manipulating the market by buying all toys from the neighbouring store), and so on (see Steyaert, 2007). They also find the right moment to act, work as a team, and manage (more or less) to deal with family concerns, albeit in a somewhat machismo, 'dare it all' manner.

This story suggests that the budding entrepreneurs saw these opportunities as existing out there, ready to be grasped. While this acknowledges that choices were not clear-cut but often driven by necessity or based on guesswork, it remains a story painted in broad brush strokes, emphasising critical junctions navigated by the cunning, tenacious, and resourceful interventions of the key players. But such stories can quickly become a bit linear and limited when they reduce the work of entrepreneurs to seeking and finding a sweet spot (an imbalance in the market) and then rely on some entrepreneurial magic to make things happen. This diminishes the task of entrepreneurship, making it primarily a search exercise while de-emphasising the whole raft of activity that goes with developing and nurturing a fledgling organisation, often navigating difficulties and changes in direction, whilst still clinging on to some sort of consistency between the beginning of the entrepreneurial journey and its successive waypoints.

This suggests that *having* certain entrepreneurial traits is not the same as actually *doing* entrepreneurship, which may very well require a combination of different skills and modes of thinking or acting in specific circumstances and situations. This seems obvious but the consequences of Gartner's little shift towards considering what creating organisations entails is profound. We cannot simply deduce from statistical characteristics how an entrepreneur will do out there, 'in the wild', as little as we can know how a football team will perform on the pitch from the mere statistics of their individual players or, closer to home, how good a lecture of an academic will be, just because they have published an important paper. A lot of intellectual baggage is piled up here. Ideas to do with traits and personality profiles are common in more psychologically focused studies. Questions of how things happen in certain contexts are often more prevalent in sociologically influenced work and, in particular, for those interested in social practices and processes. Rather than conceive of entrepreneurs as being static in their personality profiles, such approaches readily acknowledge the importance of how people may feel; how their desires change over time; how things may not only be interpreted in one way but by many and at times conflicting perspectives and so on. There is a somewhat ironic element here too, because it is precisely being flexible, nuanced, or at times manipulative when working in-between different perspectives, that can be a key element of entrepreneurship. As James C. Scott (1998) outlined, those with a lot of power, like big firms and large bureaucracies, need to draw clear lines and they require unequivocal causalities. But the world is none of these things, so those with fewer resources or political power can be flexible, nimble, and capable of coping with multiple views and unresolved differences and so often outwit those who come at things only in rigid ways. Entrepreneurship that appreciates, rather than eliminates, differences, anomalies, incongruencies, multiplicities, and the small moments of in-betweenness can, when nurtured, give rise to new ways of doing things.

This has been acknowledged in some academic accounts of entrepreneurship. Dimov, Schaefer, and Pistrui (2021), for example, point to the paradox that the more research strives to be objective and detached, and the more entrepreneurship becomes analytically broken down into opportunity structures, personality traits, cognitive mechanisms, and other archetypical identities, the further research is removed away from the first-person, lived experience of being an entrepreneur. Lived experience overflows any reductive account that links selective factors; it points to the richness and multiplicity of situational context, complex and overlapping interpretations, responsibilities, and histories experienced by living, breathing people who may have a toothache or worry about an ill family dog. This is the stuff of which life is made, and Dimov and colleagues make a fair point asking where all of that stuff goes in much academic work, and whether it's not better for researchers to speak to and engage with entrepreneurs directly than break this complexity down into simpler causal chains.

entrepreneurship as (creative) destruction

It is interesting to play Kirzner's account of opportunities emerging from market imbalances against another one which suggests that it is entrepreneurs themselves who create these imbalances. This latter view is often associated with Joseph A. Schumpeter, an economist and larger-than-life character, born into the eastern part of the Austro-Hungarian empire who popularised the term 'creative destruction'. There is much going on in Schumpeter's work, and his own ideas also shift over the course of his life. There are also many intellectual antecedents and literary currents within and against which he writes. A fuller appreciation of his influence and thinking is only possible by engaging with the history of economic theory, and in particular the many Austrian predecessors and contemporaries, as well as the American scene around Harvard which formed Schumpeter's later intellectual milieu (McCraw, 2007). We will spend a bit more time on Schumpeter because the idea that creation involves destruction has profoundly influenced not just scholarship (as arguably Kirzner's work has) but also our everyday understanding of entrepreneurship, including policy-making.

A good starting point is Schumpeter's (1947) distinction between two types of response in an economy. *Adaptive* responses occur when economies adjust to changes such as increases in population. When an industry or economy starts doing something that is outside of its usual range of operations, he speaks of a *creative* response. Such a creative response can never be understood in advance as it is not determined by pre-existing facts; it shapes the whole course of subsequent events and their long-run outcomes; and creative response has something to do with the quality of people involved in the process. Creative responses are led by entrepreneurs who, according to Schumpeter (1947), shake up the established market order by offering new products, services, or production methods. This also differentiates the inventor who comes up with new ideas from the entrepreneur who 'gets things done', which may not be anything new at all. 'Getting new things done', Schumpeter says, 'is not only a distinct process but it is a process which produces consequences that are an essential part of capitalist reality' (Schumpeter, 1947: 152). This point needs a little expanding.

In his book *Capitalism, Socialism and Democracy* (1942/2003), Schumpeter holds that while capitalism had been around for a long time, it had largely been static: consumers spent money that producers used to manufacture things and, at the end of such a cycle, no one had much left for investment. This changed with credit. Banks afforded market participants capital to invest and so to start grow, sometimes at high speeds, leading to bigger cycles of boom and bust as soon as interest rates went up, bringing inflation and some bankruptcies, followed by subsequent regeneration. Schumpeter saw the limits of the capitalist model: The initial growth was a matter for entrepreneurs, who were then followed by managers who were able to secure larger funding for bigger firms (which were also able to fund themselves). This meant that bigger and bigger firms would be able to secure larger and larger parts of the market. As capitalism has a tendency towards such monopolisation, it needs to be balanced with another form of governance, which reigns in the market and tempers the powers of these big enterprises (McCraw, 2007: 252ff). For Schumpeter (2003: 61):

> ... the actual and prospective performance of the capitalist system is such as to negative the idea of its breaking down under the weight of economic failure, but that its very success undermines the social institutions which protect it, and "inevitably" creates conditions in which it will not be able to live and which strongly point to socialism as the heir apparent.

Business cycles (covered in a separate large book by Schumpeter) were extremely important at the time which followed the Great Depression (1929–1939), and Schumpeter drew on history as well as a combination of economics and sociology to make sense of the patterns. The book *Capitalism, Socialism and Democracy* also contains a review and rejection of the then popular Marxist historical analysis, which Schumpeter saw as too simplified (capitalists who own means of production and workers and proletarians who do not). Instead, and important for our debate, large numbers of these workers and proletarians had been able to start businesses and so own productive elements themselves. This, Schumpeter suggests, was possible because of their 'supernormal intelligence and energy' (see McCraw, 2007: 349 for more points of critique but also appraisal of Marx's work). And, on a bigger scale, while the Great Depression did resemble Marx's claims of the impoverishment of workers by capitalism, depressions had come and gone before, so even on a more macro view, the capacity for renewal was what needed to be understood – and with it, capitalism's fragility leading to such cycles.

This brings us to the famous term 'creative destruction' (which he later changed to creative response), which has influenced the literature on entrepreneurship to an immense degree. Schumpeter speaks of 'creative destruction' to identify that in a stationary economy, there is merely a repetition of activity and, thus, stagnant profits. What is needed is the 'effectuation of new combinations' by stepping outside of routine developments, a new production function that lets the innovative entrepreneur earn more than stagnant profits (Balabkins, 2006). Recombination can happen in different forms: the production of a new kind of commodity, a new production method, the development of new markets or the restructuring of a business. Schumpeter (2003: 83) writes:

> ... the history of the productive apparatus of a typical farm, from the beginnings of the rationalization of crop rotation, plowing and fattening to the mechanized thing of today – linking up with elevators and railroads – is a history of revolutions. So is the history of the productive apparatus of the iron and steel industry from the charcoal furnace to our own type of furnace, or the history of the apparatus of power production from the overshot water wheel to the modern power plant, or the history of transportation from the mailcoach to the airplane. The opening up of new markets, foreign or domestic, and the organizational development from the craft shop and factory to such concerns as U.S. Steel illustrate the same process of industrial mutation – if I may use that biological term – that incessantly revolutionizes the economic structure from within, incessantly destroying the old one, incessantly creating a new one. This process of Creative Destruction is the essential fact about capitalism. It is what capitalism consists in and what every capitalist concern has got to live in.

Creative destruction is the force that sweeps out old habits like a 'perennial gale', destroying products and firms, making room for new ventures and designs. Schumpeter argues that markets can be in a state of continuous refinement – an 'adaptive response' – until innovative entrepreneurs come along and shake up the established market order by introducing new combinations of resources, production methods, products, and services – a 'creative response'. Schumpeter's entrepreneur is therefore neither necessarily a risk-taker nor does their activity need to contain new (scientific or technological) discoveries. New combinations of already existing factors (workers, practices, resources, etc.) will do just fine, which also means that it can be done by someone who does not even own the means of production. Entrepreneurship becomes a creative activity that does not merely adapt to environmental changes, but actively sets something new into motion. This also, crucially, requires cooperation and coordination between workers, machines, logistics, and so on (Hardt & Negri, 2017: 140) and also a knack for getting others to do things for you: 'Just as a sovereign cannot place a policeman behind every citizen, the entrepreneur cannot pay everyone in social and political life whose cooperation he requires' (Schumpeter, 2002/1911: 415). For Schumpeter, 'the entrepreneur and his function are not difficult to conceptualize: the defining characteristic is simply the doing of new things or the doing of things that are already being done in a new way (innovation)' (1947: 151). The entrepreneur feels 'the dream and the will to found a private kingdom'. They have the 'will to conquer: the impulse to fight, to prove one-self superior to others, to succeed for the sake, not of the fruits of success, but of success itself' and they are driven by the 'joy of creating, of getting things done, or simply of exercising one's energy and ingenuity'. This type, he says, 'seeks out difficulties, changes in order to change, delights in ventures' (Schumpeter, 1934: 91–94), which serves not just a 'macho' aim of accumulation of wealth, but the building up of social status (see McCloskey, 2006: 243). For:

> Not only with regard to the economy, but also socially the entrepreneur must be on top of the pyramid of society.... economic success will, as success in general, assure him influence also in other sectors. His voice is heard in political matters. It is inevitable: You must yield to the weight of his personality.... Much depends on him and many depend on him... Not for long can he be excluded from the leadership of processes that increasingly steer themselves toward his interest, and that of the people in his immediate command. Thus, he becomes a political and social power. (Schumpter, 2002/1911: 414)

Now we can appreciate the similarities and differences to Kirzner's account. Both Kirzner and Schumpeter reject the then (and even still now) prominent economic notion of perfect competition, whereby markets are characterised by complete transparency of market information shared by many, basically innumerable market participants. This is also called an equilibrium condition. For Kirzner, there are always some market participants who make errors, and entrepreneurs spot these to 'nudge' the market towards greater mutual awareness by exploiting and correcting them: they are 'equilibrators' (Kirzner, 2009). Schumpeter emphasises the longer-run dynamics that are a result of entrepreneurial creativity, and he articulates how creativity, boldness, and imaginativeness drive patterns of destruction and creation. A capitalist economy, for Schumpeter, is 'incessantly being revolutionised from within by new enterprise, i.e., by the intrusion of new commodities or new methods of production or new commercial opportunities into the industrial structure as it exists at any moment' (Schumpeter, 1943/2003: 31).

Schumpeter suggested that every new creation brings imperfection. We must not forget that the process of creation is a regular feature of capitalism, so market imperfections are not an exception, but a steady picture of the alternative theoretical ideas provided by Schumpeter, in which innovation is a continuous element endogenous (i.e., inherent) to capitalism itself (McCraw, 2007: 355). Hence, while Kirzner's entrepreneur takes advantage of market imperfections that give rise to opportunities, Schumpeter's entrepreneur disrupts established market structures by infusing new combinations into the economy. In Kirzner's (2009) own words, while Schumpeter's entrepreneur is undermining established market conditions, his own image of the entrepreneur is responsible for steering the economy towards an equilibrium condition. Yet, rather than being mutually exclusive processes, Kirzner (2009) believes these views are different yet complementary since they together explain how equilibrium is both achieved and destroyed. In real-life examples, as Kirzner (2009: 14) notes, entrepreneurial forces of alertness and creative destruction are simultaneously at play, such as when pioneers of the automobile industry in the United States destroyed the conventional horse and carriage industry but thereby brought the market closer to equilibrium by making better use of resources for consumers. Both Kirzner and Schumpeter's views are therefore more different in emphasis than in substance (see also Kirzner, 2009), but that difference is still worth exploring a little bit more.

overcoming

In emphasising the creative process and in characterising the entrepreneur as a special figure, Schumpeter provides us with a blueprint for an extraordinary figure driven to break out of existing constraints. We can see, for example, how entrepreneurship is linked to the notion of progress and an individualistic conception of people for whom participation in economic affairs and success in doing so comes down to perseverance, skill, and daring. Hjorth (2004: 418) speaks of the entrepreneur as a 'handy disturber of order', suggesting that throughout the 1980s and 1990s many academics, but also politicians, began to think of something called 'enterprise'. Enterprise is often sold as a panacea in a world in which large-scale production of heavy goods and manufacturing, and with it the economic and social security provided by large firms, becomes increasingly displaced from developed economies, disrupting often generational employment patterns as miners, tool-makers, weavers, machinists, or assembly workers. In the absence of big firms which could be 'managed' (and whose fate was therefore at least partially governed by politics, which could switch between capitalist and more socialist policies), the idea that people could just 'create' new value, ventures and therefore profit and eke out a livelihood (out of the rubbles of a post-industrial landscape, so to speak) was surely an alluring one.

It is easy to overlook quite how profoundly such an enterprise discourse reframes situations and even fundamental ideas and concepts of society. The unemployed become job seekers and homeless people become rough sleepers, each making a choice to either be excluded from the possibilities of enterprise or just lie in waiting for the right moment to seize the next best opportunities. Special tax regimes reward enterprising citizens and enterprising becomes a term no longer reserved for businesses, but it pervades all aspects of society: cities and councils engage in risky purchases and investments so they are not left behind to merely 'manage' or 'administrate' static bureaucracies, but become players in 'markets' (Hjorth, 2004). Public services, including health, rail or utilities, become enterprising when they tender contracts or compete with each other through new or reassembled products and services (Doolin, 2002). Anything that 'just' remains the same is now seen to lack the ambition to leave the familiar comfort zone of stagnation (Kociatkiewicz & Kostera, 2020). This also means that personal skills and characteristics take the foreground: engaging in education is a means to develop oneself (to match one's persona with the opportunities for jobs and career) and social services turn into career centres. Lifelong careers in one industry, firm or position are out and in come notions of lifelong learning, always already expecting that what has served us so far is about to collapse before long, requiring afresh the creation of value from the rubbles of one's career. The allure of the enterprising discourse in the wake of de-industrialisation and the migration of manufacturing is now rekindled as we look at robots and other automated apparatuses taking over manual labour, while artificial intelligence systems have begun producing intellectual work that was hitherto done by professionals, including academics writing papers and books.

But we are not the first to live in interesting times. From the 1800s onwards, for example, attempts were made to not just understand the massive changes that began to transform every aspect of life but to govern or 'manage' them. This period saw immense technological changes which, in turn, drew people into cities and factories, turning their backs on rural practices that were still tied to the rhythms of nature. Safranski (2002: 320) provides a vignette that may help us see the profundity of these changes. In the early 1800s, he argues, 'young people were determined to look old. Youth was considered a barrier to success'. Young men, for example, used elixirs for beard growth, squeezed themselves into old-fashioned, stiff collars, and wore faux glasses, adopting the social mores and the formal mannerisms of previous generations. But change was brewing. Its ingredients included the rise of new scientific ways of managing the growing capitalist industrial complex, fuelled also by economic theories that pitted new marginal cost benefits of mass production against old virtues of craft and tradition. Culturally, these changes played out between scientifically rational worldviews and romanticist movements infatuated with a return to nature and life itself ('*Lebensphilosophie*') whose creative and individual sensibility had, for far too long, been suffocated by the stiff collars and formal frocks of yesteryear, signifying the idealised forms and rigid rules of the 'despotisms of the past' (Nietzsche, 1996: 173). One of the intellectual sources of this philosophy of life is Friedrich Nietzsche, a German philosopher with a mighty moustache, who ended up hugging a horse and going mad. His work, in particular on the idea of overcoming the status quo, the average, and what is considered moral and normal, makes for an intriguing background for our modern understanding of entrepreneurship, destruction, and renewal. He saw that the new, machinic age was no than the old, its oppressive regime of commerce, mass production and industrialised labour merely instilling a dehumanising 'boredom of the soul' that numbs the mind and stifles its reflective and creative capacity that marks genuine human freedom (Nietzsche, 1996: 382).

Nietzsche speaks of higher men, or *Übermenschen*, which is sometimes translated as supermen, an idiom that was all too easily twisted and abused by the National Socialist ideology and propaganda machine (Reinert & Reinert, 2006). Nietzsche saw life as equal to creative potential, what he called the 'will to power', and he felt (quite strongly and expressed in the most exquisite aphorisms) that this creativity had been snuffed out for far too long by all the things that we, humans, typically hold important: that we are better than nature; the building up of material wealth; religion; and especially our values (Hjorth & Holt, 2016). All these add up to a morality that girdles life, protecting it from devastation. What remains is a life in sickly comfort, unable to manage or suspend stimulus, and so become dependent on the pick-me-ups provided by material consumption, intoxication, and beguilement with the mundane. Nietzsche speaks of 'underprivileged' existences, incapacitated and separated from nature in the wanton pursuit of fashions, order, security, and status, a human condition marked by stagnation and tethered to the status quo to whose preservation these lacklustre, exhausted and dull 'last men' devote their pitiful efforts. Not so with Nietzsche's overman, the one figure who can overcome themselves when they can leap and leave behind the enslaved morality of the 'just and the good', harboured also in Christian values, that holds them back from genuine and radical overcoming.

To overcome oneself, therefore, is also a self-obsession that finds its rupture in the act of continuous self-description which does not consider the outside world and only how one appears to oneself alone. In this, Nietzsche was perhaps the most radical proponent: '... quite aware that what counts as resolution, perfection, and autonomy will always be a function of when one happens to die or to go mad' (Rorty, 1989: 99). Nietzsche seems to wobble between two leitmotifs here: one is the idea of a superman endowed with special gifts and ambitions, the other the figure of a child, who has not yet been seduced and sedated by the stultifying expressions, mores, wants and feelings of society. It is worth noting just how radical and problematic all of this is. For one, to overcome oneself may require a new vocabulary, rather than that into which one was thrown, 'the language that happened to be spoken by the people among whom [one] grew up' (Rorty, 1989: 109). But what would that sound like if not gibberish? Perhaps a finer point is that in making oneself different from the past, one also solidifies the past as 'something' against which one's own novel creations can stand out, which makes one a builder of fixed elements, rather than an unsettling and re-describing figure (Rorty, 1989: 105).

But we can also detect in Nietzsche's life philosophy a yearning for the radical creativity of a human being unshackled from tradition and lore, and from the ideal, the safe and the demure. There is no idleness or romanticisation of nature here, but also no busyness just for the sake of business. Productivity needs to spawn change; it has to be an act of rebellion. There are echoes here between Nietzsche and Schumpeter's declaration of creative destruction. While the former would likely bristle at the latter's ideas about 'just' re-combining already existing factors, he'd probably be quite happy with a perennial gale of destruction. It is very likely that Schumpeter was influenced by life philosophy. Reinert (2006) documents a zeitgeisty resurgence of such thinking in German literature and philosophy at the time of Schumpeter's writing, borrowing especially from origin stories in early Greek and Indian mythologies. Equally, the monopolising tendencies of capitalist systems had been well understood already when Schumpeter wrote about them (Balabkins, 2006) and so, too, had the notion of the innovator, which other famous figures, including Marx, Pareto, Schmöller and others, had already theorised. Even the very notion of creative destruction is not necessarily Schumpeter's, as it was used and perhaps even invented by German economist Werner Sombart, whom Schumpeter had met in his twenties spending what we would now call a few gap-years travelling. The problem is that Schumpeter was generally coy about his sources, perhaps also due to his vain pretence of geniality, affecting an 'I don't need to work hard to be great' attitude (Balabkins, 2006; Reinert & Reinert, 2006). In this, perhaps, he was himself quite an innovative entrepreneur of his own definition, recombining existing factors into a captivating narrative, and unlike Nietzsche, for whom brooding, dreaming, worrying, loving and hating were necessary preconditions for overcoming, Schumpeter restricted his concerns to economical mathematics rather than politics or ethics. For him, it remained 'an open question if economic development will lead to social well-being or social misery' (Peukert, 2006: 224).

We might want to pause for a moment to consider once more the notion of creative destruction. The suggestion that the economy is subject to incessant revolutions and, therefore, that all aspects of life affected by economy are equally subject to cycles of stability and change gives rise to radically new questions, such as: What shall we make of those resisting changes, for example, when they lose their jobs, when they have to work in new and different ways that may affect their wellbeing, when revolutionary new products turn customers into addicts or when new business ventures threaten existing ways of living, transform nature spots into tourist spectacles, hasten climate change, develop exploitative supply chains, cause geo-political strife and so on? At the same time, where would we be if we would not have renewal, if the old guard with their stiff collars and stiff morals were to turn the possibility of a good life into a hereditary gamble, and where we would be stuck with old habits and technologies, like dinosaurs awaiting our impending extinction? What, therefore, is the balance between destruction and creation, and who decides on how much and which parts of the old have to be destroyed and who, exactly, are the winners and losers in all of this? Such questions have gained immense importance in the wake of technological advances that can, with the flick of a switch, activate ferocious atomic powers; release deadly microbes from a petri dish; or violate the privacy of billions of people whose lives are recorded by digital systems. These are no longer just questions that can be answered with economic theories; they are questions concerning morality and the emergence of the notion of creative destruction falls right into a period when the understanding of morality fundamentally changed. It behoves us to consider its utility and effects for our own, unsettled, times.

2

Mundane Forms of Entrepreneurship

social and sustainable entrepreneurship

Creative destruction as well as the idea of alertness about market imbalances are often associated with economic gain, distilled in the notion of an opportunity. The value of innovative entrepreneurship, particularly high-growth start-ups that revolutionize industries by utilizing ground-breaking technologies, lies in its ability to drive economic growth, introduce new products or services, and create employment opportunities and to offer, at least for some, the potential (in its Nietzschean inspiration) for 'authentic' individuality. But so-called 'unicorns', reaching market values above $1 billion, or 'gazelles', growing over 20% a year, are rare occurrences (Aldrich & Ruef, 2018). Viewing entrepreneurship primarily as a process of rapidly and impactfully capitalizing on the introduction of new market offerings has therefore been questioned, suggesting that the transformations brought about by entrepreneurial work ought to be measured not just in terms of profit and growth, but also in terms of the societal changes they do and can produce. While Schumpeter remained on the fence about what these changes mean for people, animals or the natural environment, many others have come to see entrepreneurship as a – or perhaps 'the' – force to do good. Growing numbers of entrepreneurs seek to create value beyond financial gains, focusing on areas such as societal wellbeing, the provision of health and social services, education, and addressing ecological degradation.

Various labels, such as purpose-driven, sustainable, and social entrepreneurship, are used to capture forms of entrepreneurial activity aimed at solving or alleviating social and environmental problems. Social entrepreneurship is often viewed as the application of innovative business methods to tackle social challenges, such as improving the lives of marginalised or disadvantaged groups, thereby integrating entrepreneurship with social impact. Social enterprises and non-profit ventures provide a wide range of goods and services, particularly in areas such as health and social care, poverty alleviation, regional development, and education. Sustainable entrepreneurship, in contrast, refers to new ventures that strive to simultaneously generate economic, social, and environmental value.

Broadening the perspective on entrepreneurship is important not only to recognise that the motivations driving entrepreneurs are more pluralistic than economic incentives but also to understand that entrepreneurship is a process of social change. This may entail establishing or transforming social structures in contexts where formal and informal cultural norms or legal rules are absent (Mari & Mari, 2009); challenging dominant ways of perceiving, imagining, and expressing identities, values and ways of living (Beyes, 2015); or overcoming constraints to develop emancipatory social structures that foster new economic and social landscapes (Rindova, Barry & Ketchen, 2009).

Conceiving entrepreneurship beyond the exploitation of profitable market opportunities often raises the question of how alternative contributions may be accounted for. One approach seeks to make the social, environmental and economic measurable, comparable, and exchangeable as a matter of valuations on a 'triple bottom line'. This maintains the idea that ventures can simultaneously make money and produce positive social and environmental impact whenever they exploit 'win-win-win' opportunities (Muñoz & Cohen, 2018) where the lucky winners are coded as profit, people and planet in a unifying valuation framework. But trying to track performance in this way is inherently tricky. While profit offers a naturally numerical basis, people and planet are not so neatly reduced to numbers, at least not without thereby also reducing *values* to *value*. Given that economy, equity and ecology are typically mutually exclusive, they are also pitched against each other, so that one wonders who of the three, profit, people or planet, may find the loudest advocates and who is likely to lose out when it comes to the nitty gritty details of it all. Then, there is the idea that the 'bottom line', an accounting concept, can act as a universal measure for all things in life. Especially when applied in struggling, underdeveloped or unequal settings, this has more than a whiff of colonialism about it (Boje, 2016) and one wonders whether the reduction of life to bottom line figures may not itself be indicative of the race to the bottom that creates many of the problems that social and sustainable enterprises end up trying to fix.

Take sustainable entrepreneurship in the form of buy-one, give-one schemes, where sales are coupled to planting trees or giving away free pairs of shoes to those identified as being 'in need'. One may feel a little uneasy about such 'saviour' approaches. More impactful has been the UK model of restructuring the National Health Service, as well as other aspects of welfare provision, towards the private sector and social enterprises, which has become a blueprint for many other countries (Teasdale, Lyon & Owen, 2018). The evaluative scales dip into both directions. One side weighs the possibility of innovative solutions created by enterprising efforts that can radically improve or cheapen the provision of social, health, development or environmental services compared to these being run by governments, trusts, or city councils. The other side of the scales is weighted with ideological commitment to commercial, enterprising and liberal ways of running things and to outsourcing responsibilities because of the belief that the market must, quite simply, produce better outcomes. This is a debate spearheaded in the United Kingdom in form of socio-political concepts such as New Public Government and the Big Society, introducing competition into the provision of public services (Dart, 2018).

There is also the question to which extent commercial revenue streams are indeed 'commercial', when a competitive tendering process merely replaces a centralised allocation of work by pubic bodies and when workers are no longer employed directly, but subcontracted to do the same job, just for less money. Or, indeed, we might ask about what counts as sustainable in the first place. Does this include large firms providing electricity, treating wastewater or collecting rubbish or plant-based food producers who strive to reduce the carbon footprint of the industry or electronics manufacturers who rely on ethically sourced materials? Or what about a company that provides online access to information or an airline providing affordable holidays for all, or an another one making profits from selling narcotics while using its muscle to keep a neighbourhood 'safe'? It's a slippery slope.

Some have pointed to the danger that entrepreneurship becomes presented as the go-to solution for the multiple and intertwined challenges faced by contemporary society, including climate change, health and social inequality. Suggesting that 'entrepreneurs will save the day' (Hall, Daneke & Lenox, 2010) because they can spot in most social and environmental issues new venturing opportunities often follows from the Kirznerian logic that identifies problems as symptoms of 'market errors' or 'competitive imperfections' that entrepreneurs can correct by offering new products or services. Some errors, however, cannot just be corrected, instead requiring systemic change, thereby addressing the root causes of prevailing inequalities and problems (see Dey & Steyaert, 2018; Hardt & Negri, 2017: 12; Hietschold, Voegtlin, Scherer & Gehman, 2023).

While these questions remain be difficult to settle, there is potential for recognising how entrepreneurship involves attempts to create a sustainable future different from the present while also acknowledging that these efforts always take place within contextually bounded situations that enable and constrain action. Such a view does not predetermine the nature of sustainable entrepreneurship but rather acknowledges that what counts as being sustainable is constantly negotiated and renegotiated as new ventures are created and when they change and grow, as an ongoing concern for what is possible to do.

There are many positive examples of such work ranging from agricultural improvements, material innovations, wellbeing, learning, or renewable sources of energy to micro-financing and the altruism, enthusiasm, compassion, and commitment of those trying to do good, often in very constrained settings which can take a substantial economic, mental and physical toll, are immensely impressive and humbling. For example, Mair and Martí (2009) show how BRAC, a leading NGO in Bangladesh, addresses the absence or ineffectiveness of social norms and legal frameworks that prevent ultra-poor women from participating in economic life. Providing not just capital or training but also health services and social development initiatives, as well as tangible assets, such as livestock or materials for vegetable cultivation, BRAC works with limited resources with a sensitivity to local routines and customs, for instance, by leveraging cultural and religious practices, such as Islamic charity norms, and involving local elites through community-based committees to develop advocacy, community mobilisation (e.g., popular theater performances), and inclusive, participatory platforms.

What counts as constituting social or environmental values can therefore be subject to heated political or public debate and entrepreneurs might find themselves amidst controversy as they strive to offer solutions – one need only think of those providing gender-affirmative or abortion services, or those using disruptive methods of activist entrepreneurship (see Dey & Mason, 2018). Activist approaches often decouple the social from the economic part entrepreneurship, considering how their work can be a force in society that challenges taken-for-granted assumptions and unlocks new understandings. In this way, entrepreneurship becomes a social force of change, that might not, or not yet, be recognised as valuable by all members of society. Sustainable entrepreneurs striving to address environmental problems, such as loss of biodiversity or emission of greenhouse gasses, might encounter a similar situation. Rather than relying on take-for-granted assumptions about what is environmentally friendly, sustainable entrepreneurs might challenge prevailing understandings of what counts as being environmentally friendly in the first place, thereby pushing the boundary for how to demarcate the category of 'sustainability' as such (Johnsen, Olaison & Sørensen, 2018).

Straddling economic, social, and environmental aims also means that social or sustainable entrepreneurs often face trade-offs and need to sacrifice some of their ambitions when they face pressures to deliver economic value or compete for contracts (Doherty, Haugh & Lyon, 2014). The most obvious one relates to the balance of profit and social investment. Take a social enterprise in the health sector, bidding for competitively tendered public services. Tendering requires a substantial upfront administrative investment as the enterprise may hire a team of business developers and finance specialists to craft competitive bids for contracts while recruiting volunteers to actually provide the services. The result are tensions between the various interests: volunteers give their time for free with the idea of doing something good when the enterprise has to keep a lid on cost by making volunteers work to contracted service levels, while also paying their managers competitive rates. The same issues reemerge when the enterprise tries to solicit donations as alternative revenue streams, and they have to justify why they limit services and pay some staff high salaries.

Drawing attention to social entrepreneurship and sustainable entrepreneurship is important for capturing mission-driven new ventures that seek to create value beyond economics. However, we should not assume that concern for social and environmental issues is exclusively reserved for a special type of entrepreneurship. Such an assumption might imply that what we consider 'conventional' entrepreneurship is somehow devoid of social embeddedness or environmental consequences. Any new venture is embedded in a social context and relies on myriad stakeholders to contribute to its success and who are, in turn, affected by the venture. This includes customers, who peruse the market offering; possible investors, who supply financial backing; employees, who contribute their expertise to build the product or service; suppliers and partners, who provide essential materials or services; government agencies and regulators, who establish the legal and operational framework; and local communities, who can influence the startup's reputation and social license to operate.

the everyday entrepreneur

While the focus on social entrepreneurship and sustainable entrepreneurship helps us reconsider *how* we look at entrepreneurship, shifting from its economic domain towards more broadly being a social change process, we also need to reconsider *where* to look for entrepreneurship away from flashy, radically transformative, particularly risky or frenetically growing examples. The majority of entrepreneurial activity is of an everyday nature and happening in a variety of sectors, and so often lying outside of the view of the growth-hungry venture capitalists whom we will encounter later (Welter, Baker, Audretsch & Gartner, 2017).

Recognising everydayness means appreciating that entrepreneurship can take place in multiple contexts and across time (Wadhwani & Lubinski, 2017). Welter and colleagues (2017) have done much to shine a light on mundane aspects of entrepreneurship, suggesting that 'everyday entrepreneurship' is everywhere, making up the millions and millions of entrepreneurs, who do sometimes remarkable but often quite ordinary things, many of them for a long time, before handing their business to others to continue. Everyday entrepreneurs run corner shops, restaurants and groceries; they are booksellers, bakers and (as the rhyme goes) candlestick makers; people who clean windows and manicure gardens; specialist producers of metals, plastics and fabrics; tailors, child minders and hairdressers; pet sitters and dog groomers; and taxi operators, artists and agents, and they include very large, often family-run businesses such as those in the German *Mittelstand*. More recently, we have seen the mushrooming of small-scale, often labour-intensive enterprises, such as craft beers or artisan breadmaking. These are often made possible through the use of shared spaces and sharing of knowledge, facilitated, inter alia, by open-source software and freely available digital media (peer to peer) connections where know-how and resources can be shared (Arvidsson, 2020). Some of these may not have great growth aspirations and some are driven by lifestyle choices; many of them engage people who eke out a living working long hours, often doing what they enjoy and are good at, but rarely making the headlines while thriving within an environment to whose flourishing they contribute.

We may be deceived into thinking that this 'everyday' form is a less successful kind of entrepreneurship, lacking both in the fast-moving growth of their business, outside investment and the lustre of fame and wealth. But their economic impact is enormous when we add them all together (Aldrich & Ruef, 2018). And not just that, such kind of entrepreneurship provides an important logistical and social function, stepping in where the state, large institutions, or big firms don't show interest or are slow to act. Small shops pop up to extend supply chains to remote villages; independent restaurants emerge around university campuses to cater to international student tastes, often repurposing or refurbishing existing venues; and small engineering outfits produce spare parts or customisations that are no longer lucrative for original equipment manufacturers to pursue.

This echoes some of Kirzner's ideas about entrepreneurs fixing market imbalances, but there is also an intriguing self-organising logic to such everyday forms of entrepreneurship. This has long been recognised by those studying how cities work. For example, the Canadian writer Jane Jacobs, as well as French sociologists Michel de Certeau and Henry Lefebvre, have each compared how planned approaches to 'running' a city run against the sheer complexity of the myriad processes involved (Beyes & Holt, 2020). Just imagine an inner-city shopping arcade. Early in the morning, there will be deliveries for newspapers and magazines as well as fresh produce which has to be purchased from markets and shipped to the arcade; others will finish off sweeping the street while window cleaners begin their work. Some of those working in shops will have dropped their children off at enterprising nurseries, whereas others will have arranged dog walkers to visit their homes during the day. Repair workers will be scheduled to attend to faults in the buildings that someone has identified, with some luck being covered by an insurance purchased from an independent financial broker. Even before any shop opens, there is an immensity of overlapping, temporally sensitive and multiply connected things to prepare for, organise and cobble together in the moment when someone is ill or when a delivery fails to arrive, or the millions of other things that happen every day, over and over again, in every arcade in every city.

To frame how things can get organised without there being a central, overarching or controlling organisational element, Certeau distinguishes a view from 'below' on street level from a view from 'above' like when one looks down at a busy city from a high building. However hard one looks from up there, one can never have complete oversight, since there is always an alleyway, a shortcut, a hidden path and a boundary from where people and things pop in and out of vision. Lefebvre draws a distinction between different aspects of space, one being the space that city or town planners envisage (similar to Certeau's way of looking from above), and then there is a kind of space as it is experienced by those living in it. Jacobs, finally, is quite cross with such planners who look from above and carve a city into islands, separated by multi-lane highways cutting through neighbourhoods or when they develop housing estates where each window faces inwards onto a private garden, rather than outwards, where the hustle and bustle of a well-functioning community happens. Certeau, Lefebvre, and Jacobs have in common that they like messy stuff and that they think that throwing oneself into the mess actually works much better than making abstract plans that tidy up the muddle, at least when it comes to complex affairs such as a city or an arcade. Lefebvre even has a label for this: *lived space*, which suggests that self-organisation can make a space alive and flourishing, well beyond what one could plan in advance or from the outside or with a view from the top.

Our little detour is helpful to think about the role of entrepreneurship in this logistical and social sense. Big companies, institutions, councils and other bureaucratic entities require planning cycles, forms to be filled and signed, large orders to be placed, and targets for employees set well in advance so that their contributions can be measured. That can make such organisations sluggish, and it can make them hesitant taking on small or odd jobs. This is where entrepreneurship can come in, providing local or small-scale solutions to problems and helping to create order from noise without any centralised or orchestrating influence. Self-organisation harbours the idea that components of a system influence each other, directly and immediately, so that in the event of a disturbance, they can recalibrate how the overall system behaves. In the 1960s there were even concrete plans build self-organisation into a city's physical architecture. One project was called the 'Fun Palace', a design for an arcade that would 'continually reconfigure itself in relation to the shifting needs and desires of its inhabitants' (Pickering, 2010: 366). Part of the problem of self-organisation, however, is that it is by no means clear how, why and when it works. Scientists have, for example, developed mechanical tortoises made up of self-organising parts, while others have won Nobel prizes for identifying the thermodynamical physics of self-organisation in liquids. But that is still a far stretch from the self-organising that goes on in an arcade which is a complex mix of materials, technologies, humans, and other creatures that produces and maintains itself by creating its own parts, thereby also creating something more complex than the mere sum of these parts. It is intriguing to think of entrepreneurship in this way. If we add up the many, many entrepreneurs all doing such small bits of work, we very quickly end up with a big system that works without any central figure being in total control or charge of it or having complete oversight. Everyday entrepreneurship and the beehive-like complexity of the many interacting entrepreneurs now look quite impressive.

Understanding entrepreneurship in terms of not fully formed, articulated or indeed not yet visible elements also points towards activities that are merely possible but not yet real, or others that are undertaken in the shadows and grey areas, outside of regulations or laws and away from the public and academic gaze. Such forms of illegal and at times criminal entrepreneurship range from small 'off-the-books' tax infringements to hardship-driven forms of entrepreneurship, including more or less organised practices that fund or supply abuse substances, right up to complexly structured mafia-type organisations that mimic legitimate corporations with hierarchies, hiring processes and cost accounting departments (Smith & McElwee, 2014). Even when entrepreneurial work is not outright illegal, it can still be morally questionable.

Examples include a startup selling vapes, importing bottled water from the other side of the planet, selling unhealthy and addictive fast foods or getting customers hooked on gambling or alcohol. The matter becomes even more complicated in terms of technological innovations that generate the possibilities for zero-hour contract work, surveillance practices and data harvesting for targeted advertising, or those that fill social media echo chambers with commercial or political messaging, which may be just ahead of the law or operate within the parameters of neoliberal free-market ideas but do so while producing detrimental social, economical and ecological 'externalities', including cultural and mental devastation.

Everyday entrepreneurship also concerns forms of activity grounded in necessity and we can observe big international differences here, relating to the distribution of wealth, institutional support and structural constraints (Martinez, Jayawarna & Marlow, 2024). This includes employment options for immigrants and marginalised, geographically isolated or stigmatised groups and also those excluded from wage employment, those whose wages are insufficient to sustain them and their families and those opting out of salaried work, innovation or technologies as a token of resistance (Juma, 2016), such as entrepreneurial punk bands and rural and communal entrepreneurship ecosystems (Drakopoulou Dodd, 2014). Imas, Wilson, and Weston (2012) use the concept of 'barefoot entrepreneurs' to explore the entrepreneurial practices and narratives of individuals living in marginal, poor, and excluded places. They study how people in deprived areas of Chile, Argentina, Zimbabwe, and Ghana undertake entrepreneurship from the margins, challenging conventional ideas about who can start a business and which principles and values are associated with entrepreneurship. Emerging in peripheral contexts, entrepreneurship can help foster social transformation by organising solidarity and community, creating economic opportunities and social wealth, addressing socio-economic problems in less competitive, destructive and selfish ways and promoting a different language of entrepreneurship, which explicitly includes varieties of cultural and institutional contexts (Holm & Beyes, 2022).

Appreciating the everydayness of entrepreneurship also nudges us to reconsider the notion of opportunities with which we started. Schumpeter had already pointed to the collective, not just individual ways in which entrepreneurial functions are filled. Gartner's (1988) catchy notion of entrepreneurship as being the creation of organisations invites us to further consider the often basic and tedious things required when moving from an idea to actually putting in place organisational elements. It also points to the specificities of the situations in which all this happens, and the many and varied structural, cultural, historical, temporal, or material aspects that affects them. Hidden behind the statement 'entrepreneurs create organisations' lies also a perhaps somewhat cheeky tautological loop – it is like saying 'footballers create football games'. The statement does not really yield a direct answer, but it is an invitation to ask further questions: What is an organisation? What do we mean by creating? When does creation stop and turn into mere management? Is the entrepreneur an entrepreneur before they create a business? Dimov (2020: 343) suggests we should think of opportunities more broadly as 'situation[s] in which it is possible to do something'. Now that's quite broad and inclusive. It includes a fast-growing venture, but it can also involve simpler aspirations to gradually build a venture that solves a problem for potential consumers, such as opening a bakery or coffee shop where none existed previously. This definition also quite cleverly adds the notion of a 'situation' which is always a specific moment in time and in space. This suggests that it may be tricky to try and calculate an opportunity from a distance, away from the space in which its possibilities lurk. It also suggests that opportunities are time-sensitive. We may think back here to Certeau, Jacobs and Lefebvre who also had a sense for timing, and for the coming together of rhythms that give some spaces a vibrantly buzzing aura or, alternatively, as rhythms that slow down and peter out, like the declining waves of tourists frequenting the domestic seaside resorts forgotten in an age of cheap overseas holidays. Such broader notions of opportunity therefore shift concern from specific instances to situations, which are marked by broader social and economic patterns that shift over time. Everyday entrepreneurship therefore also points us to the general surplus value that is generated in entrepreneurship beyond exploiting a momentary market disequilibrium. This can be the way that someone can do something that was not previously possible or solve a problem in a more convenient way, or it may refer to the accumulation of entrepreneurial activity contributing to the rhythms that animate a city or district, with whose wellbeing they are inexorably intertwined (Ramoglou & McMullen, 2024). Finally, speaking of what is possible, Dimov also points to the unfinished nature of opportunities, and that they require some doing to gain shape and form, for only then can they be recognised as being this or that. The notion the opportunity continues to be a central concern for many academics studying entrepreneurship but it also seems clear that however we define 'it', we create as many insights as we do problems.

A few authors, including Popp and Holt (2013), Dimov (2020), and Ramoglou and McMullen (2024), have tried another tack by asking what the word opportunity means, not as an abstract concept, but in the sense of its use in everyday language, and how it helps entrepreneurs and academics to navigate life. Calling something an opportunity is helpful when it allows us to get on with things, like one builder saying to another 'hand me this brick', and recent studies have looked at how the term is used by entrepreneurs to express visions of future ventures, thereby expressing their confidence in the existence of conditions that allow them to act for the purpose of realising a desired future state (Dimov, 2020; Ramoglou & McMullen, 2024). This, then, shifts the focus towards how entrepreneurs act forward by using language to convert what *they* consider an idea for a new venture into what is a venture recognised by others. But when the word becomes cumbersome because we spend ages trying to define or measure it, and it starts getting in the way rather than letting us get on with things, we may have to drop it and get back to words that are more usable. Some have indeed suggested that it would be better to simply discard 'opportunity' altogether, while others have strived to rehabilitate the concept by offering alternative views on how to understand the nature of opportunities.

the entrepreneurial society and the creative class

In addition to the literal meaning of everyday entrepreneurship as engagement in mundane ventures, it is intriguing to consider how entrepreneurship or, rather, a narrow notion of enterprising has encroached on our everyday lives as a style or habitus that reshapes how we think of ourselves and the world around us. Let us, for a moment, tune into the messaging of innovation and management guru, Peter Drucker. Drucker envisages the 'entrepreneurial society' (2015: 313ff) whose ingredients include the breaking up of unions, tax breaks for startup companies that would also be able to charge the state for bureaucracy inflicted upon them and generally the 'need to encourage habits of flexibility, of continuous learning, and of acceptance of change as normal and as opportunity – for institutions as well as for individuals'. The latter in particular:

> can no longer assume that what they have learned as children and youngsters will be the 'foundation' for the rest of their lives. It will be the 'launching pad' – the place to take off from rather than the place to build on and to rest on. They can no longer assume that they 'enter upon a career' which then proceeds along a pre-determined, well-mapped and well-lighted 'career path' to a known destination – what the American military calls 'progressing in grade'. The assumption from now on has to be that individuals on their own will have to find, determine, and

develop a number of 'careers' during their working lives. ... And only they themselves can take responsibility for the necessary learning and re-learning, and for directing themselves. Tradition, convention, and 'corporate policy' will be a hindrance rather than a help. (Drucker, 1985: 325)

Hardt and Negri (2017: 210) coming from an orthogonally opposed perspective comment that, for Drucker, '[w]orkers in a neoliberal entrepreneurial society are essentially bird free, that is, free from stable employment, welfare services, state assistance – free to manage their own precarious lives as best they can and survive. What lovely hypocrisy!'. But it seems Drucker got it right, even if we may contest that this means the right thing has come to pass. Andreas Reckwitz, in his book *The Invention of Creativity* (2017), similarly notices how an initially liberating ethos of creativity has become accompanied, if not hijacked by new forms of coercion that involve a frenetic level of activity geared towards the production of continuous aesthetic innovation where each new cycle is momentarily captivating but ultimately unsatisfying. More on that later.

Drucker's outline of a self-motivating and self-updating workforce was written against the backdrop of the decline of industrial production in the United States and Europe and the spectre of the displacement of blue-collar work through automation and robotisation in manufacturing. Focussed on industrial production, such 'old' forms of work carried a spirit of regularity, rationality and efficiency, a form of capitalism that has as its blueprint the large organisation and as its operator the figure of the administrator or technician. Since the 1970s, however, much work has changed into what Richard Florida (2002) has called the 'creative class', which produces new routines, texts or objects, to foster and satisfy a consumer body yearning for novelty and change. This 'creative ethos' geared towards the production of continuous novelty is not restricted to the manufacturing of industrial goods but, as Reckwitz (2017) illustrates, also – even predominantly – applies to the arts, fashion, education, architecture and thus to culture on a broad level. As such it is both an expression of want and desire but, operating at the level of culture, novelty also becomes a characteristic that is socially expected. This shift is accompanied by sweeping changes in the ways value is understood. Rather than objective price setting (e.g., by a state) or adding up costs, such as materials and labour, plus profits (as in labour theories of value), the development of marginal cost theories turns the question of value into a matter of subjective consumer preferences. This means that the value of a consumer good is divorced not just from how much it costs to produce but also from any objective notion of utility or scarcity. Instead, we enter a phase in which commodities are aesthetically loaded: they become objects of changing consumer fashions and their value is tied to their perceived novelty which, in turn, is judged in terms of the excitement they induce (Reckwitz, 2017). Aesthetically loaded commodities are unmoored from any fixed social context and, instead, traded individually and embedded into a lifestyle where consumers can appropriate a commodity by loading it with subjective feelings. They can even become objects of idolatry, fetishised as autonomously desirable objects or vice versa, loathed when they are deemed unfashionable.

As there are multiple ways in which value can be created, there are consequently also multiple ways for entrepreneurs to produce something new. Reckwitz, once more, is helpful here as he distinguishes three different kinds of novelty: *The new as a step-change in human development* (novelty I); *the new as heightening and supersession* (novelty II); and *the new as stimulation* (novelty III). To these, we will add a further one (novelty IV) in which the *new refers to the generation of a medial surround* in which consumers live cosseted by data traces they leave behind which are fed-forward into predictable and controllable behavioural patterns.

We already got a sense of *novelty I* in the writings of Nietzsche, who is after a profound set of changes, nothing less but a new way of understanding the self which, in his writings and through his literary protagonists, he preaches to the crowd of the unreformed. For Reckwitz, radical novelty is concerned with the transformation of deep-seated structures that mark a new stage in the development of society. In this, we are also reminded of Schumpeter's discussion of the shifts between capitalism and socialism as political governance structures that set the arena for entrepreneurial commerce and conduct.

Reckwitz's second form, *novelty II*, is one of continuous, and more gradual development. We may think of computer transistors or mobile cameras that follow linear or exponential curves of 'improvement' with no end (or 'stage') in sight. This is still a production-centred form of novelty, driven by pricing, engineering and research, and aspiring to a version of humanity as well as prosperity that keeps on going up as time goes on. Here, we can already see what Günther Anders (2016: 43) calls the 'conventional perversion' of novelty, by which it is no longer demand that leads to supply, but supply producing demand as a secondary product.

When we come to Reckwitz's *novelty III*, we find that any (objective) notion of improvement has fallen away. Novelty and value are purely a matter of temporary consumer tastes. Here, for example, we find the introduction of 'inessential' aspects into technological products.

Cars that were initially designed to get us efficiently from A to B are now laden with gimmicks or stylistic features that weigh down the once efficient solution. Consumer 'choice is now exercised under the dubious influence of charm, prestige, flattery, of all the social myths or personal faiths', while bloating the vehicle, making it heavy and inefficient (Simondon, 2012: 11). In such cases, Reckwitz speaks of aesthetic novelty, which is concerned with the production of stimuli alone. This aestheticisation of commodities is also seeping into other aspects of life, and now we have artistic, economic, media-related, cognitive, gastronomic, educational and urban practices that continually seek to excite. Everywhere we now find creative people working hard to keep up the levels of surprise and unpredictability, without the requirement for the 'new' to be better than what was there before.

But there is perhaps even a *novelty IV*, one which exceeds Reckwitz's notion of the aesthetic in which we still find the human being as the subject of supply and demand. The fourth kind of novelty turns the consumer into an information/production complex whose every moves in digital networks or, physically, in 'smart' homes or 'smart' cities, produces surplus information that is harvested for targeted advertising and behavioural influencing. Anders (2016: 43) suggests a new form of perversion that now posits machines the centre of such subjectivity:

> The *machine* now openly and shamelessly presents itself as the '*subject of desire and demand*'. It demands to be offered what it needs and expects that humans exert themselves to come up with ever better offers (because humans in their present state are not acceptable to machines). Humans are thus required to supply everything the machine needs to function as well as it 'could' function.

We may be a little bemused by Anders's science fiction style talk of machines, but we have to remember that he started to think about this from the 1930s onwards. Now we would speak of surveillance capitalism (Zuboff, 2019) enabled by the continous tracking and computational pattern seeking enabled by smartphones, the internet of things, body trackers and implants, augmented realities and gamified interfaces, which all work on the human body to no longer arouse aesthetic attention, but to change the behaviour and, increasingly, change the human mind–body complex itself. This fourth kind of novelty turns the consumer into the product by harvesting information that is then computed and fed back to the consumer, often bypassing conscious awareness. Here, the human being becomes a by-product as well as being co-opted into a regime of processes that keep on rattling, computing, producing and consuming, requiring of us that we submit to being analysed and continually 'improved', as if to make up for the 'shame' (Anders, 2016) of being born naked and wrinkly, generation after generation beginning from scratch, while machines just keep on developing.

These four types of novelty are helpful for our discussion of entrepreneurship because they allow us to qualify the notion of creativity. *Novelty I*, concerned with a radical revision of structures in stages, sets a tall order. It is clear that such novelty cannot be sustained on a continuous basis, neither collectively as the fabric of society needs to be woven into at least somewhat continuous strands and patterns, nor individually, lest the skills that come with the continued refinement of work, including the capacity to calculate and mitigate the risks and adverse effects of doing business, as well as identities, plans and ideals, are continually disrupted or discarded. Such continued radical transformation would require higher-order form of learning, which Gregory Bateson (1987, ch: 4.7) identified not just as the challenge of learning new things (already a step up from learning how to do the same things), but to learn how to learn to do new things all the time. As Bateson has shown, this can be a frustrating and alienating experience, and we may rightly wonder how such an exceptional idea can become standard. *Novelty II* involves the generation of new features that keep on improving some aspects of life. We can see this form of novelty in early phases in new technological developments: combustion engines become more efficient or faster; batteries last longer and extend reach; computers more powerful; university programmes more professional; and so on, but we also see how that it may be tricky to keep a healthy payoff matrix between the investment required to continuously becoming 'better' and the utility of such improvements for users or consumers (another few megapixels on a phone camera; another top speed record for a car). *Novelty III*, on the other hand, explains how consumers can be motivated to keep on spending money on new things because the real utility of a purchase stems from the excitement of having or experiencing it alone. This form of novelty also chimes with Schumpeter's definition of entrepreneurship as the recombination of factors, as long as they produce something that stimulates an audience. This is just recombination (Schumpeter), a tireless form of labour, without the need to overcome the present (Nietzsche). Schumpeter is worth quoting at some length here (2002: 408/9):

> You can always have the new combinations, but what is indispensable and decisive is the act and the force to act ... It is this type that scorns the hedonic equilibrium and faces risk without timidity. He does not consider the implications a failure ... or care

whether everybody depending upon him will lose their keep for old age. He does not care at all what his equals and superiors have to say about his enterprise, and his daily work has not left him without force and courage. And whatever his situation, whether he urgently needs further employment, or can abundantly satisfy all his needs – he is tempted by the act. The decisive moment is therefore energy and not merely the "insight." The latter is much more frequent, without leading to even the most simple act. What matters is the disposition to act. It is the ability to subjugate others and to utilize them for his purposes, to order and to prevail that leads to successful deeds – even without particularly brilliant intelligence.

Novelty IV, finally, is less clear as we are in the middle of an unfolding experiment around us. As McCloskey noted, easy access to affordable technologies has played a big role in allowing many more individuals than ever before to produce goods and offer services. But especially collaborative and creative digital tools also siphon off data, turning not just end-consumers but also the entrepreneurs themselves into 'products' whose information is then being sold on for marketing and other purposes. As Fisher (2018: 493) has it:

The good old days of exploitation, where the boss was interested in the worker only to the extent that they produced a commodity which could be sold at a profit, are long gone. Work then meant the annihilation of subjectivity, your reduction to an impersonal machine-part; it was the price that you paid for time away from work. Now, there is no time away from work, and work is not opposed to subjectivity. All time is entrepreneurial time because we are the commodities, so that any time not spent selling ourselves is wasted time.

Hardt and Negri (2017: 211) suggest that this resembles, 'at its lowest level, a bureaucracy of one, a structure of individual self-management in which it is difficult to distinguish freedom from constraint' (Hardt & Negri, 2017: 211). This is of course well known, and Schumpeter had it covered when referring to the social status of entrepreneurs to attain free 'social labour'. Hardt and Negri (2017: 141) once more:

recognizing that the cooperation imposed or required by entrepreneurs takes effect not only in their factories but across society, over populations paid and unpaid. Social labor, in addition to being unpaid, must also be functionally subordinated and ordered toward a specific productive goal. This is precisely the hypothesis that, during the years of the crisis of the Fordist industrial model, led to practices of externalization, along with the diffuse factories and construction of complex industrial zones that supported a new social organization of production.

What seems to be clear is that this is not a welfare state approach (such as that by Gustav Schmöller) but a mathematics-based understanding of how capitalism mediates and alters the patterns between production and consumption. Next, we will look at how a specific set of business startup approaches have turned the dial even further by transforming the distinction between suppliers and customers, so that the latter comes to supply information, feedback and even free labour to the former. We enter the age of the experiment.

3

Entrepreneurship as Experiment

the Silicon Valley–style entrepreneur

Let us turn to the rogue, geeky, going-against-the-grain genius misfit. A university dropout who risks it all, epitomising the American dream by journeying from rags to riches. Rocking up to business meetings in sneakers and T-shirts, this entrepreneurial figure ends up winning bigly against the odds and then basks in the display of luxury, lavishing in the conspicuous consumption of private jets that carry them to private tropical islands where they host hot celebrity parties. We, too, become part of their success when their bright smiles shine from glossy magazine covers, and we can enjoin hordes of social media fans following, liking and retweeting even their most banal or offensive comments in the idle hope that we may imbibe a little of the aura of success that the entrepreneur so evidently possesses in excessive abundance.

This not-always-exaggerated image of the Silicon Valley–style startup founder has come to occupy an outsized chunk of our imagination about entrepreneurship. But this is not the only reason we will spend a bit more time on this style. We have to acknowledge that entrepreneurship fusing contrarian countercultural ideas with computing technology, bio and health sciences and a hyped-up form of capitalism has been perhaps the most transformative force in our lifetime. As Barbrook (2015: 11) has it: 'The [internet] was creating a "new paradigm" of global entrepreneurial capitalism which would soon sweep away the state regulations and bureaucratic monoliths of the industrial epoch'. We now see tech startups that have never made profits and that, at times, don't even have a revenue plan, being valued in multiples of (old) industrial multinational corporations that have built up capital, expertise, routines, products, patents, customer relations, brands, trust, and social capital. We see such new ventures creating surplus away from products and services by capitalising on the information traces we all leave in virtual or surveilled physical spaces.

Combined into computational patterns, they allow for targeted predictions of consumption behaviour, auctioned in real-time to advertisers (Zuboff, 2019). And we see startups providing infrastructure to nation-states and pan-national institutions that now, in turn, rely on the goodwill of entrepreneurs for access to satellite information, software patches that keep critical services free from malware and hostile intrusions while providing assistance in moments of crisis, when vaccines are needed or solutions to climate change have to be articulated to a voting public without, however, restricting or incumbering freedoms or standards of living (Farrow, 2023).

The basic scheme of this form of entrepreneurship begins with a superb, often radical and certainly disruptive idea. In its most basic form, such radical disruption was made possible by the emergence of the Internet, which enabled a 'paradigm of global entrepreneurial capitalism' (Barbrook, 2015: 11), epitomised by the Silicon Valley entrepreneurship ecosystem, which has given rise to digital platform ecologies, artificial intelligence technologies and the computerised development of bio and health sciences, which in turn have created immeasurable wealth and previously unthinkable technological breakthroughs.

This new paradigm is not geographically restricted to the San Francisco Bay Area. The idea(l)s that entwine entrepreneurship with technology as a fundamentally disruptive force has sedimented into many policy decisions about how to support the creation of startups, and many newly elected politicians flock to California, bringing back initiatives to transform an ailing region, or a struggling economy, into a similarly money-printing structure. There are now IT clusters in Germany's Rhine-Main River area, the region between eastern Denmark and southern Sweden has been called the Medicon Valley, or even the whole of Sweden has been labelled a new Silicon Valley, as has the United Kingdom, or at least the areas connected to London. Technology startup programmes are regularly taught at many universities which also host spin-off labs, incubators and other commercialising setups, and startup entrepreneurial idea(l)s are now woven deeply into the expectations and dreams of students across the social and natural sciences. Somewhat invariably, the entrepreneurial format is one in which a budding entrepreneur 'pitches' a business idea that can be scaled quickly to a multitude of markets and applications to a group of investors. These provide funding, social network access and mentoring to take the idea global with the aim of creating a company that can be floated on the stock market. Audretsch (2021) suggests that Shane and Venkataraman's (2000) individual–opportunity nexus equally derives from the idea of innovative tech-based high-growth ventures, indicating the centrality of the notion of payoff for investments.

And, so, we keep marvelling at the pace at which inventions and innovations come at us, transforming life as we know it: travelling, dating, investing, paying, making art, consuming the 'news', cultivating friendships, teaching and learning, and especially buying stuff keeps transforming in rapid cycles. But not only have we benefitted from immensely innovative products, it is now possible for all of us to get into the business of doing business ourselves because more and more people are part of the group that owns cheap and powerful means of production. All you need is to be online and have a mobile phone camera, a 3D printer, access to a large language model or any other now cheaply available bit of kit to become your own boss. These more recent technological developments continue and intensify a longer pattern. McCloskey & Mingardi (2020) identify a period of 'great enrichment' from 1800 onwards in which the ordinary person was liberated from the yoke of institutional constraints. It is a time when '[o]rdinary people, emboldened by liberalism, ventured on extraordinary projects (2020: 31). It is the point where 'creative innovation' was placed in the hands of everyone, not the state and not just a select few with the means or the hereditary rights to commission expeditions or inventions, and whose preferences, as we must assume in any case, lay with preserving the status quo (and their position in it) and not with change. Most interestingly according to McCloskey and Mingardi, ordinary people benefitted the most, seeing their lives improve manifold.

But for all these improvements, there is a lingering sense that the great enrichment has been quite an uneven affair. Wealth is concentrated in the hands of a few, geographically, but also in terms of a new stratification of workers. On top is the 'virtual class', a bohemian set of business founders, programmers and investors, whose particular ideological blend mixes hippy idealism; hyper-capitalism; resistance to rules, governance and authority; and an unbending belief in the possibility of overcoming limits, extending even to the 'transhuman' effort to prolong human life, eternally. A lot of this was captured in the notion of 'the Californian ideology', coined by Barbrook and Cameron (1996). This ideology has developed and continues to propagate a quite specific set of idea(l)s about how life ought to be lived and governed.

Before we get to this, it is worth considering for a moment how the immense success of a new technology venture is made possible. If we look at a manufacturing, craft or service-based business, we can imagine that growth requires many small steps. It starts with having a business to begin with, one which produces things or provides services, for which the owners or managers of the company see a growing market. They may then plan expansion by adding product lines; producing more batches; perhaps working multiple shifts; and hiring, training and integrating new staff, who need to be there a while to build up mutual trust and a functioning organisational culture, as well as an enlarged human resources department and various rounds of recruitment, each one requiring the drafting job adverts, running interviews and onboarding activities. The firm may buy new machinery that needs to be integrated into workflows and customised, and staff need to become competent at working with them, which, in turn, may mean facilities may need to be expanded or changed.

Service organisations too, when expanding, will need to train their staff not just to provide the actual services, but in the use of client management software, policies and practices, and they may have to carefully manage the introduction of new staff into existing client relationships. The firm may even consider relocating to a geographical area where skilled labour is available, or where land is cheap or where suppliers are favourably located or where infrastructure requirements are met, which is all very capital-intensive, requiring detailed planning and project management, engagement with local policies and laws and so on. Then the firm has to negotiate loans or other forms of investment to cover all the expenses, for which they typically have to produce business plans demonstrating promising sales and profit trajectories, and then negotiate internal politics when it comes to deciding what exactly to do and how much risk to take. All this is disruptive to the existing business. Edith Penrose (1995), in a remarkable book first published in 1959, outlined how growth means that current productivity will drop as existing staff will have to spend time recruiting and training others, and then carefully delegate tasks before they can turn to the business of growing further. Matters get even more complicated when we then look at international expansion, which involves legal, cultural and language-related challenges, as well as dealing with logistics in a world that sees growth in regulatory barriers and shifting geo-political contexts.

Looking at these examples, we may recognise that not all businesses lend themselves equally well to rapid growth of the kind that turns a startup into a globally disruptive enterprise that manages to also make money. The ones that do seem to be quite similar: fast-food chains that redeploy standardised workflows, workplace designs and menus; they pool supply chains and marketing; and spread the cost of expansion through franchise models, thereby rapidly covering large markets. Retailers who repeat their schemes internationally can expand quickly by drawing on complex logistics to exploit efficiencies of scale and scope. But all this still requires a lot of human intervention: negotiations, contracts and planning, and so on.

However, what really has the potential for expansion are digital matchmaking platforms, such as those for homeowners to rent out their private dwellings for tourists and travellers; platforms allowing you to use your car and your own time as a taxi service; an app that allows anyone with a bicycle and a smartphone to become a food delivery agent; more apps that provide platforms for temporary work, art, banking, music, insurance brokering, dog sitting and connecting sellers and buyers of new and used equipment; and so on.

We may note a few commonalities here: these are often ideas that involve business models in which the absolute bulk of the work is not done by the employees of the business, but by a mix of customers and co-producers: Airbnb does not provide its own rooms or bedding; Uber does not own fleets of taxis; Facebook does not upload its own images or stories. Instead, these businesses act as brokers or orchestrators who bring together 'pro-sumers' who both produce the content for the platform and who also are customers of such content. This outsourcing of production to the consumer has a few decisive advantages: digital platforms only need to hire small numbers of employees to keep the technology going and to provide basic central functions, such as marketing and legal. They can add hundreds or hundreds of thousands of users, who populate content themselves, without really requiring that much more effort. This limits the involvement of the technology business to running servers and providing, typically, a very basic set of services, often further outsourced to automated BOTs, FAQ sections or forums in which users help each other. The keeps the cost of doing business, also called 'transaction cost', very low, while growing the business requires little extra investment.

While these digital platform businesses are perfect vehicles for growth models, they have one decisive disadvantage: they don't provide straightforward revenue models. The need to 'scale' relates to what is called the 'network effect', which suggests that the value of a platform directly derives from the size and growth of the user base and the amount and quality of the things they add to the ecosystem. But this means that membership or transaction fees are detrimental as they are a hindrance to user and engagement growth. Examples of how profitability can be achieved include platforms starting off with free services, before adding advertisement and premium subscription options. They may also offer specialist services that may have a temporal advantage where, for a while, they can charge fees and continue to grow, at least as long as they maintain their specialism advance. A platform may also have exceptional market power or be so central in the orchestration of the ecosystem, for example, by controlling platform technologies or connected logistics processes.

But we can also see that even extremely successful platforms struggle to monetise their models without, at the same time, driving users to other 'free' alternatives.

Once we ask how a digital platform can generate consistent revenue, we can detect a second cycle that lies behind the producer–consumer one. It begins with a redefinition of the product. While the producer–consumer relation is based on users uploading images or text about themselves or about services or products they want to offer or acquire, the second cycle turns the 'pro-sumer' into the product by harvesting the data provided (as well as data about interactions and related activities) which can then be monetised, for example, by auctioning it to advertisers for targeted marketing approaches. This second cycle explains why tech firms invest billions to develop products and services they provide to us 'for free': access to music, maps and routes, creative tools for videos or do whatever else we want. As the saying goes: if a service is free, you are the product.

We can now come back to the question of what this means for entrepreneurship. On the one hand, we have massive potential payoffs (remember the private jet flying to the private tropical island for that exclusive celebrity party). On the other hand, it is also clear that there are many barriers to things really 'taking off' and to keep on growing until there is enough momentum that revenue streams outweigh the initial and ongoing investments into the design and maintenance of the technology, but also the marketing that is needed to keep growing. Peter Thiel, himself a former entrepreneur associated with PayPal and now an investor in startups and political ventures (we will hear more about him later), readily accepts that only a vanishingly small number of business startups make it into the business stratosphere. Entrepreneurs who rival movie stars in fame and who sit at the helm of organisations that are astronomically valued, at times irrespective of the revenues and profits they produce are, by the very nature of being so special, quite few in numbers.

To understand this logic, it is helpful to look at a quaint little book on entrepreneurship written by Thiel (2014: 105ff), which outlines the 'power law of venture capital'. Venture capitalists raise funds from investors, looking to identify good firms into which they can invest, hoping that these will become more valuable. Venture capitalists take around 20% margin and often operate on 10-year investment plans. However, as most startups fail, venture capitalists need to spread their investments, and here's the rub. Thiel suggests that there is no one-to-one correlation between growth in value and firm quality. Having a portfolio with a 33:33:33 split of good, mediocre and failed firms will not yield a sufficient balance of profit or value.

Venture capitalists are therefore doing badly when they hope for a random distribution of success/failure that will naturally yield a balanced portfolio. Such 'spray-and-pray' approaches to investment are poor because what venture capitalists need to identify are not 'good' companies that can potentially generate a 2x or 4x return on investment, but rather companies with tremendous growth potential. What Thiel calls the 'power law' is this: 'a small handful of companies radically outperforms all others' (2015: 85).

This is perhaps a version of the Hunger Games, where the road to riches is littered with disappointment and failure of the many which then still pays off for those investors savvy enough to spot one of the few that make it. The enlightened investor does not 'spray' money all around and instead tries to identify those rare 'beasts' that survive the feeding frenzy. Such high-growth firms are given names such as 'gazelles' which, in nature, are graceful creatures belonging to the antelope family. A few successful ventures should not only cover the potential loss of the remaining ones but also generate the return on investment that they have promised their limited partners. In entrepreneurship lingo, the total addressable market must be substantial enough for investors to envision the potential for breakout success.

The way this works is that investors place capital in startups in exchange for equity, meaning that the investors gain ownership or control while the entrepreneurs' shares get diluted. Investors may also join the company's board or have a say in its composition. The endeavour is often a successful 'exit scenario', such as the company being merged or acquired by another investor or company, or that the startup is publicly listed on a stock exchange (known as an 'initial public offering'), so that the initial investors can cash out by selling their shares for a higher price than what they initially paid. As startups are typically cash flow negative, meaning that they spend more money than they generate, capital from investors is crucial for these startups to grow. There are many good reasons why gazelles are compared to entrepreneurial growth patterns. They are resourceful: as they live in waterless regions, they had to adapt and, instead of drinking, they are able to extract moisture from plants. They are also resource-preserving: extracting water from their urine and excrement. Gazelles are also nimble: relying on their speed to escape predators and they can do something called 'pronking' which means jumping in the air and kicking out with all four legs at the same time. Gazelles are highly sociable: baby gazelles, called fawns or calves, can stand up minutes after being born and they can run soon after. Fawns seem to also have found a place in online gaming, but that's another story, and there is even a creative element here, as the word 'gazelle' stems from the Arabic language, originally meaning 'love poem'. Gazelles belong to the entrepreneurial zoo of metaphors along with mice, black swans, unicorns and other more or less fantastical beasts, growing in number and adding to confusion (Aldrich & Ruef, 2018). The reason for this sprawling fauna is that there are many entrepreneurship commentators who mainly or even exclusively value high growth and highly capitalised startups, which are typical for the Silicon Valley type of entrepreneurship.

And as we have already suggested, also those responsible for policy decisions as well as those tasked with implementing entrepreneurship training – including many universities that now offer entrepreneurship programmes, outreach teaching, mentoring, incubators and spin-off facilities for the commercialisation of research, based on different private–public partnership arrangements in accordance with prevailing varieties of capitalism and governance models – have tried to replicate the gold rush in their own backyards (Baker & Welter, 2024). Governments around the world have poured much money, time and hope into emulating the conditions that made Silicon Valley a hotbed for transformative innovations, economic growth and, let's not forget that, geopolitical influence by providing key technologies that underpin commercial, administrative and defence systems and services worldwide; bio and medical technologies to deal with climate change, population growth and viruses; and artificial intelligence developments that fundamentally alter the nature of work, promising radical changes to the international competitiveness of a nation (Casper, 2007). Governments have therefore attempted to foster attractive clusters (see Audretsch, 2015: 8) via subsidies and tax breaks that lure complementary firms to settle in specific regions, or by creating or attracting more of the creative class people by investing in universities or international talent programmes.

business models and the lean startup

Given the importance placed on fast-growing organisations, it is of little surprise that there are many recipes outlining how such startups can be cooked up. One is to look at them as nascent organisational forms. We have already come across a few key characteristics of this idea: an assumption that a startup is 'just' a large business in a larval stage, and the associated suggestion that the move ('scaling') from small to big has to be done quickly with the aim of gaining a dominant market position, to exploit first-mover advantages and, in the context of digital platforms, positive network effects. Such a process is not profitable but costly and it requires major investment provided, for example, by angel investors or venture capitalists, who bet on a few extraordinary winners while accepting that the majority of firms in their portfolio will fail to reach the top.

This gives a central role to the matchmaking process between those who generate ideas and those who invest, and especially the 'pitch' has become its go-to format, attracting, in turn, much attention by academics, in airport books and also in TV shows. The word pitch suggests a piercing movement, driving in a stake, and that is what those seeking to 'land' investors are trying to do in extremely competitive, highly ritualised and immensely compressed settings (Clarke, Cornelissen & Healey, 2019). In such fever-point environments, entrepreneurs must convey the right information and pitch their business idea comprehensively, outlining its basic architecture and how will it create value and for whom (Chesbrough & Rosenbloom, 2002). Given the need to cover all the basic aspects of a newly proposed business in the short time of an investor pitch, many start-up recipes prescribe a fairly standardized 'business model'. Business models suggests, on the one hand, that there are a key elements that every business needs to consider, build or implement. In considering, collecting feedback and rearranging the basic architecture of their business before it is built, the entrepreneur can question basic premises early on. Business models still represent a key pedagogical artefact in many entrepreneurship courses run by business schools. This involves students having to sketch out a series of 'hypotheses' (see Blank, 2013) relating to what the new venture will do (its activities), who it will work with (partners), the resources it requires, which customers it serves and how it builds relationships with these, which channels of communication, sales and logistics it develops, how it organises its cost structure and how it generates revenue streams. Such hypotheses can then be neatly plotted onto a pre-formatted and freely downloadable 'canvas' pro forma, so that teachers or potential investors can see, at one glance, whether the budding entrepreneur has done their homework and connected the dots.

This all sounds tremendously commonsensical with a whiff of scientific experimentation thrown in, but there are various issues to consider. Models, including business model approaches, represent 'small world' versions of 'large worlds' (Ehring & Foss, 2022). They are handy because they reduce the complexity of the real thing by expressing some of its structures, objects or processes in a new medium that, unlike the real world, can easily be prodded, observed and reconfigured. Such a concern for itself means to use it as an 'object to inquire into' (see Morgan, 2012: 31). This is a concern with how the model itself works. The much more difficult Part is trying to use models as 'objects to inquire with', which means drawing inferences from the small world of the model to speculate about how the 'large world' of real life may operate. Part of the problem is that there is no objective way of creating a model. Models are made and used by people who have their own experiences, preferences, perceptive capacities, intuitions and expectations, which form the basis for decisions about what goes into the model and what is excluded, and how its various parts may interrelate. As Heinz von Foerster (2003: 283) reminds us: everything said is said by an observer to an observer; which is a clever way of saying it takes two to tango: that a model does not represent an outside world as much as it reflects the biases and blind-spots of entrepreneurs and investors who draw up models to communicate with each other.

For example, are entrepreneurs and investors best viewed as standing outside of their models, or should they see themselves being inside them, and so having to consider how any particular model affects their own capacity for action and knowing? What about the idea that businesses can be viewed from above, in all their complexity? Or what about the implicit notion that businesses can be modified at will; that their parts can be rearranged as easily as one redraws a line on a piece of paper? What about the contextual variables that may mean that in some situations particular solutions may work when these very solutions, at other times, may be the sources of new problems? Or, finally, what about all the things that are small, seemingly insignificant, less obvious or difficult to measure that are necessarily excluded from a small-world model? This may include 'tacit' forms of knowledge, such as one's ability to hold casual conversations or 'knowing' from the sound of a machine if it is about to develop a fault; social relations that require the development of trust; or the emergent and self-organising features we mentioned earlier.

Business model approaches may be interesting for investors like Peter Thiel, whom we encountered earlier, when they are trying to pick the few winners from a large pool of potentials. It is an efficient way of seeing in a quick and ready fashion whether anyone asking for money has at least thought it all through is a helpful minimum expectation. Business models lack, however, in being based on hypotheses about what an entrepreneur thinks their organisation may do or encounter before actually doing it, while the clarity and neatness of pre-designed models may mean that they will find out the hard way that reality is, in most cases, quite different.

In the winner-takes-it-all approach, all those startups that get their hypotheses wrong are lost cases, and this seems pretty wasteful. What is missing is a way of utilising all that failure (after all there is so much of it around) in a productive way. This is the subject of what is called 'lean' startup approaches, championed by Steve Blank and by Eric Ries, who

has written a best-selling book with the same name, as well as popu-
lating an influential blog. For Ries, a lean startup is an organisation
designed to create new products and services under conditions of
extreme uncertainty. In such conditions, hypotheses about the elements
of business models are unreliable. Rather than first designing the startup
in minute detail and then implementing the design to see if it sinks or
swims, lean startup is all about trying things out straight away, and
making the smallest steps possible. For Ries (2011):

> Startups exist not just to make stuff, make money, or even serve
> customers. They exist to learn how to build a sustainable business.
> This learning can be validated scientifically by running frequent
> experiments that allow entrepreneurs to test each element of their
> vision.

A lean approach is therefore not primarily about having a good idea,
spotting a great opportunity, having particular entrepreneurial traits or
scaling from zero to one in the fastest possible time. It is, if we follow
Ries, not even primarily about the hypotheses about customers, revenues
or partners one would plot onto a business model canvas. Instead, it's
about learning based on a method inspired by scientific practice: a
'build–measure–learn feedback loop' intended to turn hypotheses, based
on founders' previous experiences and which are largely just 'guesses',
into facts (Blank & Dorf, 2012).

Gregory Bateson (1979: 194) offers a helpful distinction between two
kinds of error correction either in the single act or on a class of actions.
The first happens when entrepreneurs gather feedback in the early stages
of ventures, perhaps developing prototypes or running ideas past
potential customers, like a marksman with a rifle may look down the
barrel and continue to correct her aim before shooting. The second is
more like shooting a revolver from under a table, where the shooter has
to rely on skills she has acquired prior to pressing the trigger, for
example by practising on a large number of dummy targets in this way
to calibrate the *setting* of her muscles and nerves. In lean approaches the
error correction happens not in one single action but in a large class of
actions, with customers as dummies.

Out, therefore, goes the attempt at developing a complete and
finished product and in comes the 'minimum viable product' (MVP), a
stripped-down version of the market offering that contains just enough
functionality to be convincingly presented to early adopters, thereby
allowing feedback to be gathered from them. Electric car companies, for
example, implement on-going product changes, rather than packaging
these into distinguishable facelifts and generational new releases.

Software companies typically ship products that are already in need of upgrades and patches by the time they leave the factory without ever endeavouring the completion of a finely tuned and balanced product at a final point as the next stage of development, and so the next MVP, is just around the corner. Out, therefore, also goes the idea of a homogeneous product line which was still the hallmark of mass production and in come deliberate variations to test differentiated customer reactions.

effectuation

Where the lean startup literature is based on the experience of its key authors who legitimise their claims through their personal successes and compelling stories from practice, a related approach with very well-developed intellectual roots is called 'effectuation'. Sara Sarasvathy (2001), who came up with this term, suggests that most entrepreneurial firms are not fully set up from the start: they are not sure about their long-term strategic goals, they have no existing personnel, and therefore no routines, culture or processes, they may even be in an entirely new industry where there are no standards or recipes for how to get things done. Or what, even, if one wants to start an organisation that defies any existing form – what about a firm that does not want to grow or even follows a de-growth ideology? How, Sarasvathy asks, does one recruit new staff to such a firm? How does one set a strategy if one is not clear about one's aims and values? How does one develop products and think about quality, price points, margins and overheads? How does one get investment if there are no formulae or existing data on how such a firm would perform? Such complex, messy and unclear situations call for something different to rational thinking and to the many economics-derived formulae and analytical techniques which were (and perhaps still predominantly are) what Sarasvathy saw business schools teaching on entrepreneurship courses.

Sarasvathy happened to work with some of the most profound thinkers on the limits of rationality in economics and business studies, Herbert Simon and James March. Key tenets of rationality include: starting with knowing one's aims (and keeping such preferences set stable), knowing all the possible options available as well as the outcomes (or utility) of each of these options, and then having a way of comparing these objectively (for example by their profit value). A rational decision is therefore a process of calculating the best possible option before acting. Note that the setting of aims and the process of choice (that is the calculation of options) are entirely separate. Note also that aims do not (or cannot, in the rational model) change. And finally note that there is no room for anything else to change: options cannot suddenly be worth more or less; the mode of calculation cannot just move from looking at profit towards things like beauty; and each option can only have one specific outcome, and not be dependent on many things that may happen as time goes on. In a way, the rational choice model is very good because it allows economists (and economically minded business scholars) to focus their attention on calculating the best means for realizing a given end. Just assume that goals are given, various optional available, and you are off. Running a business becomes a matter of processing information about possible pay-offs and risks associated with various choices to arrive at the optimal course of action.

But, similar to the lean startup authors Blank and Ries, Sarasvathy points out that this is far from what happens in any business, never mind small entrepreneurial ones. This is where Herbert Siomon, a Nobel laureate and pioneer of artificially intelligent systems, comes in. Simon had developed a design approach to complexity derived from biological systems which, he argued, are built up of systemic parts which are variously nested ('loosely coupled'). There are, in other words, hierarchies in nature that we can take as blueprints when it comes to dealing with our limits of rationality. Simon (1996: 188) provides us with a parable of two watchmakers (whom he calls 'Hora and Tempus', the first word meaning a time span such as an hour, but also a circular dance, while the latter perhaps indicating a more linear, ongoing time), each making highly complex watches. Hora prospers, while Tempus's business falters. Why? Tempus works sequentially, producing one watch at a time. But as his business grows, he finds that he is interrupted a lot, and each time all the pieces he has so far assembled fall apart, meaning he has to start the whole process again. Hora, on the other hand, recognises hierarchies and modularity; he goes around in circles, compiling each complex watch from sub-systems, with lower complexities. So, when Hora has to put down a partly assembled watch to answer the phone, he loses only a small part of his work. Simon speaks of 'nearly decomposable' systems in 'which the interactions among the subsystems are weak but not negligible' (Simon, 1996: 197), such as the connection between a task completed prior to picking up the phone and the subsequent one that is thereby interrupted. Hora even manages to assemble his watches in only a fraction of the man-hours it takes Tempus (Simon, 1996: 188). There is a nerdy quaintness to Simon's writings here, displaying as part of his arguments against purely rational logics a curious commitment to the rationality of numbers, when he follows this example with a minute quantification of the differences in complexity and risk, ending with the claim that 'Tempus will complete an assembly only 44 times per million attempts $(0.991000 = 44 \times 10\text{-}6)$, while Hora will complete nine out of ten' (Simon, 1996: 189).

This brings us back to Sarasvathy who develops Hora's mode of working, as the identification of hierarchies and near decomposability has profound implications for how agents design systems. For one, it suggest that the system does not need to be understood in its entire complexity (an insight Simon developed into the concept of bounded rationality), as it is sufficient to be concerned with problems on a mid-range level – parcelled into manageable frames, for which 'satisficing' solutions can be found. This implies that organisations can expand human rationality *qua* symbol processing (Mirowski, 2002: 454–7). Second, it means that heuristics can be optimised using symbolic routines ('expert systems') which work within given frames (but without questioning those frames themselves, or being concerned with the complexity of the entire system).

For Sarasvathy, entrepreneurs do not start with an idea of where they want to be (what in 'causal' language is an 'effect') and then assemble the 'means' to get there (that was, after all, the recipe for Tempus's ruin), as this would require the capacity to predict (see 'hypotheses' in lean startup thinking), rationalise or control many complex factors stretching into the future. This is of course impossible; but what is possible – and here Simon comes in – is to create smaller and less complex sub-systems, which are sufficiently de-coupled from their context. Mimicking Horus, entrepreneurs can, over time, put together relatively simple sub-systems and compilet hem into a more complex organisational wholes. The brilliant thing about Sarasvathy is that she provides a very hands-on way of talking about this: start with the smallest sub-system, which is you, and the means you already have and see what you can do with these. Then, add a new sub-system by asking others to join in with you: customers or suppliers, competitors or anyone else with whom you can find some shared purpose. This requires legwork and mouthwork. The effectual entrepreneur will be out and about, talking to people rather than hypothesising things from home. Once you have someone to collaborate with, gain their commitment. This is where the magic happens: once you collaborate with others, you will gain access to new means, but it may also require you to change your existing goals, to accommodate those of your new collaborators. This takes you back to the beginning or, rather, to the beginning of a new cycle in which you can once more speak to others, commit them and see what means you acquire and how your goals may have to change. If a new cycle (or a new sub-system with new collaborators) does not work out, you can go back to the last step just like Horus did because you haven't placed all your eggs in one basket.

Sarasvathy provides a welter of examples and easy-to-remember formulas to liven up this process, and she emphasises that, rather than biting off too much in one go, you can work within an expanding circle of means. The acknowledgement that goals and purposes are not necessarily clear from the outset is a key aspect of design approaches and different design traditions have come up with principles for the movement between parts (sub-systems) and wholes to get from abstract sketches, concepts or artefacts to more concrete ones. Design approaches are therefore also particularly interesting for entrepreneurship, which often faces uncertain, risky or unknown environments (Berglund, Bousfiha & Mansoori, 20220). Changing goals and means as you go along is therefore absolutely fine – Sarasvathy calls this exploiting contingencies – as this allows for the gradual expansion of complexity (Horas outdoing Tempus), as long as you keep an eye on where all this means–ends maneuvering takes you, for you may not feel comfortable changing some goals or accommodating those of new collaborators. Effectuation completely reverses the logic of rationality, which big firms often use in their strategic decisions. Most entrepreneurs start out with little, so they don't have many resources to fight competitive battles. What they need is ways of leveraging the bits they do have – and then making the best of them. This means pooling resources where possible, finding partners to share risk, cost, access to finance or resources and much more. This is another way of saying that when life hands you grapes, make wine. In this way, by framing entrepreneurship as what you can afford to lose rather than a calculated return on investment, and as a process rooted in who you are rather than a meticulously crafted business model, effectuation broadens access to entrepreneurship, making it viable within resourceful as well as constrained contexts.

risk and myopia

But let's return to the tech-based, high-growth potential forms of entrepreneurship that proceed on the basis of testing and scaling a new business model. Here we come to the downsides to some of these experimental forms of entrepreneurship. One is that while failure is common in entrepreneurship, not all failures are positive learning experiences (Olaison & Sørensen, 2014). Another is that the reliance on technology and science can happen at the exclusion of much else. Rapid scaling requires disruption which, at least for the last years, has typically been based on technological advances such as the many digital platform-based startups, and the bio and medical sciences that dominate the Silicon Valley. Many of these startups swallow up significant upfront investment, for example, by competing for talented workers, and so require a constant stream of investors ready and able to take the gamble. Given the importance of technology and science for governments, there is also typically a strong dependence on government funding and policy, for example, by underwriting research at institutions such as Stanford, but also via direct commissioning of work or work and research collaborations especially by the defence sector (see Galison, 1994). Such focused dependencies mean that changes in government policy, including the perceived nature of threats, as well as changes in the investment climate can have momentous influence on the entire sector.

Another downside relates to the question of what we may call myopia, groupthink or more broadly 'culture'. On a basic level, and as the Silicon Valley example shows, a buoying technology sector can crowd out other sectors simply based on the cost of living and studying, researching, as well as doing business in radically gentrified milieus. Then, there is the question of to what degree a relatively tight-knit community of investors and entrepreneurs is susceptible to hypes and excessive risk-taking (Manjoo, 2022). Current examples include Web3 crypto developments, such as non-fungible tokens (95% of which were reported as being worthless in 2023) (Yang, 2023), as well as crypto exchanges and funds such as FTX (which filed for bankruptcy in 2022 leaving some $8 billion of debt), or the health tech company Theranos (which had raised some $700 million in venture capitalist funding and was liquidated in 2018), or even the relatively offline world of the office rentals company WeWork (listed in New York, which had managed to attract over $10 billion in investment and was valued at nearly $50 billion but filed for partial bankruptcy in 2023).

There has, of course, always been a consideration of risk in entrepreneurship and even prior to the arrival of venture capitalists, technology startups were supported by federal agencies and laws that mitigated risks (Adams, 2021). Frank Knight, as early as the 1920s, associated entrepreneurial rent (profit) with risk, as did Kirzner, whom we encountered earlier, while the wages of the labourer are guaranteed but also limited. Knight (1921) adds a helpful qualifying element, namely uncertainty, which is a factor suggesting that there are types of risk for which not even probabilities can be calculated (we may think of spreading certain risks by investing in portfolios or buying insurances). Radical uncertainty is the domain of entrepreneurship because the only way of mitigating risk is judgement and instinct, and it is with these abilities that entrepreneurs can transform uncertainty into profit.

Venture capital is the flipside of the entrepreneurial element, providing funding with no necessary expectation of immediate return, and a positive attitude to chance and risk. A series of interviews conducted by Sally Smith Hughes (2009) with an early venture capitalist, Reid Dennis, are instructive:

> Well, the broker would call us and say, "Would you talk to so and so." And then one of us would talk to him and get a preliminary idea and then we'd say, "Well, we'll call the group together. Can you join us for lunch on this or that or some other day?" ... He would tell us his story and after lunch was over – and it was always a he – he didn't get much to eat, but nevertheless, he'd get the story out. We'd excuse him and say, "Go stand outside on the sidewalk for ten minutes and let us talk about this and we'll come out and tell you what our decision is." And we'd talk around the table – "Do you like it? Who has questions?" And so forth and so on. "Who's going to be on his board?" We'd assign one of The Group to be the leader and then we would go out and ... we'd tell the ent[repreneur].

Interesting is not just the gender and geographical exclusiveness but also the lack of prudence in decision-making which other investors, such as pension funds, would have to legally apply. What moves to the forefront in such situations is therefore the personality of the entrepreneur, their charisma and vision when they construct a story of a venture in the short performance art that is the 'pitch'. This is especially true in the seed financing stage, where risky startups often lack a proven business model. Venture capitalists understand that the financial projections presented by entrepreneurs in their pitches are often speculative, so while the plans may be wobbly, the focus turns on those presenting them, and how credible they sound. Entrepreneurs therefore typically sell a vision for the future, and investors evaluate their confidence in the entrepreneurs' ability to bring that vision to fruition. The overreliance for decision-making on the entrepreneurial figure has taken on near cultish dimensions. Once more, examples abound. WeWork's Adam Neuman was credited with a bombastic persona and outlandish storytelling abilities, being 'too charming for his own good' (Wiedeman, 2020: 1). His charms worked on Masayoshi Son, a Japanese billionaire and founder of the software distribution giant Soft-Bank, who had made (and lost and remade) his money with risky investments, including Alibaba, the Chinese online retail giant. He had done so after meeting its founder, Jack Ma, and reportedly seeing 'the sparkle in his eyes', which reminded him of Bill Gates, Steve Jobs and his own being 'a little crazy' (Wiedeman, 2020: 123). In 2000, Masayoshi Son set up a $100 billion vision fund, and in their second meeting, he made up a contract awarding $4 billion in funding to Neuman's WeWork in the back of a car they shared following a reported 12-minute pitch by Neuman (Wiedeman, 2020: 133).

It is worth, once more, to return to the idea of a Californian ideology, as outlined by Barbrook and Cameron in 1996, which already spells out some of the underlying inconsistency between the idea of an exceptional, creative, daring, 'crazy' entrepreneur who single-handedly creates a startup from nothing and the fact that it is taxpayer money that largely funds university research, defence and infrastructure contracts (see also Galison, 1994), and in particular early computer development schemes; taxpayer money also supports the development of high-speed computer connections; state support for key electronic and biological industries while warding off global competition, courts and law enforcement for property protection and countless hours of free time offered by pro-grammers but also others who develop code, moderate user boards and provide product reviews; and once more, taxpayer money is used to deal with externalities, such as the contribution of the energy consumption of 'proof of work' blockchains to climate change. At the time of writing, it was estimated that the bitcoin network alone consumes 174TWh of electricity a year, exceeding the use of a developed and industrialised country such as Poland.

But there is also another inconsistency, because what appears to most people as 'crazy' is seen by those 'in the know' as being entirely rational: 'The rationalist worldview was the idea that nothing not social niceties, not fear of political incorrectness, certainly not unwarranted emotion could, or should, get between human beings and their ability to apprehend the world as it really is' (Burton, 2003: 6). This includes questioning things that 'non-rational' people take for granted: that death is really inevitable, that cars cannot run on batte-ries, that a few committed and 'effective altruists' cannot change the world, or that democracy is really the best political order. Questioning basic foundations is to act against habit and bias and thus against what 'indoctrinates' us: the deep state, the media, or just our laziness of thought. Great breakthroughs come when we question what others take for granted. This 'going against the grain', not trusting authority or public messaging, is deeply rooted in counterculture which has translated, via hackers of telephone networks and computes into (transhuman) hackers of the human body and (neo-reactionist) hackers of the political order (Turner, 2006).

what's it like to be an experimental entrepreneur?

It is also worth moving back from these exalted examples to the everyday experience of entrepreneurs, and the way the Silicon Valley model configures the status of life and the human. Such a biopolitical or bioethical question opens up when we look at the pressures for conformity to identity stereotypes moulded by expectations of genius, self-sacrifice, and radicality. The average work-week in such startup communities habitually exceeds 80 hours, typically with little pay but the prospect of future stock realisations. Add to this reportedly high levels of harassment, misogyny and psychological stress, and within a highly selective gender, race, age and socio-democratic profile of well-educated and well-connected competitors. And then there is the pressure for 'affective labour'. As Mark Fisher (2018: 493) astutely attested:

> Being exploited is no longer enough. The nature of labour now is such that almost anyone, no matter how menial their position, is required to be seen (over)investing in their work. What we are forced into is not merely work, in the old sense of undertaking an activity we don't want to perform; no, now we are forced to act as if we want to work. Even if we want to work in a burger franchise, we have to prove that, like reality TV contestants, *we really want it*. The notorious shift towards affective labour in the Global North means that it is no longer possible to just turn up at work and be miserable. Your misery has to be concealed – who wants to listen to a depressed call centre worker, to be served by a sad waiter, or be taught by an unhappy lecturer?

It also points to the growing genre of self-help books and seminars, as well as those providing help to fortify and augment the human body and mind for seemingly *superhuman* achievements, delivered with an upbeat voice, a well-trained body and frozen smile. More geographically specific, perhaps, is California's hippie and counter-culture movement, with its attempts at consciousness expansion through drugs such as LSD but also its appropriation of spiritual practices such as yoga and meditation, and its entanglement in early cybernetics. We therefore also have a culture of self-finding spirituality and related practices that lend corporate missions an often cringeworthy messianic fervour while providing individuals ways of coping with the prevailing uncertainty and pressure.

While some might find deep passion in engaging in such forms of entrepreneurship, for others, including us, this sounds like a deeply stressful way of living, and we may ask the question of whether the prospect of future riches for a few outweighs the pain and trouble of working in such a hyper-capitalist milieu. Mark Fisher (2009: 36) speaks of 'hedonic depression', a schizophrenic double-bind by which wellbeing is associated with material affluence and such affluence being accessible to anyone by virtue of sheer hard work, ingenuity and tenaciousness. But this is of course not so: upward mobility has stagnated while mental illnesses are on the rise. It also begs the question of how far is far enough. James March already stated that great hopes lead to great disappointments and to the sacrifice of human decency and honesty (Augier, 2004). We may therefore also wonder where the entrepreneur is in all of this: we have investors who pick ideas; we have those purveying them; and we have then organisational structures that boost any company that makes it through. No one sticks around. The thing scales up and is then sold, made public, and so autonomy is given away. Let's go back to Thiel (2014: 115) who suggests:

> You should focus relentlessly on something you're good at doing, but before that you must think hard about whether it will be valuable in the future. For the startup world, this means you should not necessarily start your own company, even if you are extraordinarily talented.

We are left wondering whether we still really talking about entrepreneurs who make things themselves, and whether, instead, we should see entrepreneurs as speculators or investors who back the right horse. This would also explain why we find so much entrepreneurial talk revolving around pitching, whereby those who 'produce' variety are brought together with those capable of 'seeing' what is really new or worth developing – with the latter, the investors, being the 'real' founders, as only they have the foresight to envisage the opportunity that arises before them – already formulated and partially developed by others who are mere innovators. It also reinforces the assumption that the only entrepreneurial firms that 'count' are those that fit into a high-growth, highly captialised frame, such as the fabled 'gazelles' which scale rapidly, adding revenue, workforce and value, even if not necessarily profit, in their early years. Many of the key technology companies started out as fawns, 'pronking' around their territory until they found sufficient investment to grow into household names such as Apple, Dell, Yahoo, Meta, Cisco, Microsoft, Amazon, or Alphabet/Google.

Before we move on from the Silicon Valley, there is just one more consideration to include. Because we are now in an era where social relations, the private sphere and free time are the products and the source of monetisation, so that almost everyone now can be or already is an entrepreneur. It is a shift in which the self becomes an enterprise, and individual autonomy, which had hitherto been a source of opposition to neoliberal and other forces, now becomes a source of commerce, turned into clickbait and revenue streams. Not only does this turn all social relations into competitive ones, it also produces a radical version of what in Germany is called the *Ich-AG*, the self as enterprise in which one's own wellbeing, wealth, health and happiness depend on how well one 'manages' to extract value from one's life. This, as McNay (2009) identifies in Foucault, is not a homogenising demand but one that produces a multiplicity of differentiated enterprises, each eking out a living just at the margin of what individual autonomy yields: first you rent out your flat when you are away, then a room permanently, then the sofa in the hallway and so on.

techno-progressive entrepreneurial politics

There are a few corollaries to this experimental approach worth exploring, as they help us understand more about a new form of entrepreneurship which emerges in progressive technological contexts which harbour more or less explicitly acknowledged political tendencies. First, there is especially in 'lean' approaches an intriguing shift from the old idea that organisations produce goods to satisfy consumer demand towards 'users' on whom products and ideas are being tested in iterative experimental cycles, making the business the consumer of information. The involvement of customers (as well as other parties) in on-going product design processes, which is often mediated by new communication technologies, has become known as 'open innovation'. Effectuation, with its focus on joint commitment and shared goal development, has the potential to be much less one-sided. Berglund et al. (2020) distinguish lean and effectual approaches in such terms, suggesting the former uses experiments (e.g., with customers) to discover and clarify uncertainties in the environment, while the latter is more transformative, using negotiation to construct new realities jointly.

Second, and equally driven by information technology, is an accompanying tendency for businesses to analyse their customers. This has taken on such importance that products and services, which made up exchange relations in industrial forms of capitalism, now become secondary to information gathered about consumers. In particular, software-based offerings, apps, digital platform services or programmes are frequently available 'for free'. Some of these are open-source developments, while others are made available by businesses trying to gain market share with the aim of charging money later. Many others, however, are never intended to make money directly, but serve bait to catch consumer data, which are the new commodities in a new political economy which Shoshana Zuboff (2019) identifies as 'surveillance capitalism' and which we earlier sketched out in terms of *novelty IV* as the *generation of a medial surround* that turns consumers as well as entrepreneurs into products.

Third, this touches upon interesting links to various, seemingly oppositional tendencies. One is the idea of continuous improvement and problem-solving, but also the very idea of freedom that characterises the 'Californian ideology' (Barbrook & Cameron, 1996), which is borne out of pioneering communities that fused anti-authoritarianism and counterculture with self-help science. An early example is the *Whole Earth Catalog*, which published product reviews and advertised DIY 'tools' for self-sufficient, ecological and holistic living which was part of a technologically savvy community aiming to create alternative models for social change through entrepreneurship and technology (Hepp, Schmitz & Schneider, 2023). Another is rooted in Austrian economists' anti-communist sentiment, whose mistrust of the state and, more broadly, forms of communal collectivist processes, has made it into varieties of libertarianism and neoliberalism as well as more recent alt-right anti-globalisation movements, which also feed from Christian fundamentalist aversions to meddling by the state or other public institutions, perceived to have a left-wing bias (Doody, 2020).

Against this backdrop, it is interesting to hear Google's Eric Schmidt or Meta's Mark Zuckerberg declare that they are not in the business of making money, but to 'make the world a better place' and to 'solve global problems', respectively (Morozov, 2013). Such solutions include the internet of things, which coordinates your shopping; online maps tell you not just how to get somewhere but, by learning from you, also where to go in the first place. University students have large language models ghostwrite their essays, and we can order meals from our sofas, to be delivered via a competitively priced network of freelance workers who, we must presume, prefer cycling through the fresh city air whenever *they* want to do a job rather than being encumbered by old-fashioned things like pensions or sick pay.

But there is a further, and more sinister element here too, harking back to the notion of overcoming which we earlier traced to Nietzsche. For example, Google's Director of Engineering, Ray Kurzweil (2005), who labels himself 'author, pioneering inventor, and futurist', developed the notion of 'singularity', which holds that computers will become as smart as humans, who in turn will live forever. The analysis of these historical and cultural links goes beyond the scope of our book, but what intrigues us is the emerging role of the entrepreneur in such techno-optimistic, transhuman, solutionist and above all libertarian accounts. It combines the view that all aspects of life can be understood in terms of problems for which technological solutions can be found with a belief in the ingenuity of select individuals to come up with the right solutions. In combining technology, commerce and a mission for change, the entrepreneur is exemplified in popular culture and science fiction through the figure of the space pirate or the hacker, a rogue and independent player who takes on the establishment to solve the problems that states and formal institutions create. It is worth noting that these solutions often involve the augmentation of the human body, just as the prowess of the entrepreneur itself is based on rigorous regimes of self-improvement, be it through spiritual practices, vitamins or implants.

What emerges here is a radically politicised version of entrepreneurship that combines visions of social change with the modification of human bodies which, in turn, become a site of experimentation. This takes relatively benign forms, such as when technical (digital) networked devices, such as Amazon's Echo, are capable of understanding certain queries and so, over time, change human speech patterns towards command-style instructions. In a wider sense, it implicates 'users' into what the philosophiser of technology, Simondon (2012), calls their associated milieu, by making user input part of the functioning of the technology. But, as Hernan and Ramirez-Figueroa (2021) note, such modifications appear to be part of a wider ideological design programme with eugenic overtones, geared towards human progress and betterment by large Silicon Valley tech firms. This takes the form of investment in biotechnology startups attempting to slow human ageing or develop DNA-based advertising, but also, and here we come to the sinister bit, as part of a wider intellectual programme associated with a number of academics and, increasingly, freelance philosophers associated with post-neoliberalism, neo-reactionary, Dark Enlightenment and accelerationist ideas, which are funded and broadcast by Silicon Valley startup billionaires. Such ideas are geared towards destabilising the capacity of governments and formal (public) institutions to govern and instead replacing these with a renewed assertion of the authority of private ownership and governance. Davis and Gane (202: 10) span an arch from Austrian neoliberal and paleoconservative figures such as Hayek whose concerns for morality were rooted in individual responsibility rather than collective and government-led forms of 'coercive

enforcement' to von Mises and his follower Rothbard; the latter's infa-
mous notion of the state being 'the organization of robbery systematized
and writ large' has done much to fuel current libertarian and Alt(erna-
tive) Right thinking while the (media) strategies of right-wing populism
involve the denunciation of state institutions and functions by turning
'treason into virtue' (Cooper, 2021: 39).

It will be the job of entrepreneurship historians to trace in more detail
the interconnections between the technophilic entrepreneur and the
political programmes, social and religious trajectories, as well as
geographic, migratory and colonial patterns that lurk behind the shiny
products and squidgy-clean personas of the Silicon Valley and beyond.
We may also connect these last points back to Reckwitz's outline of
different kinds of novelty. Singularity, solutionism and trans-humanism
are aimed at the improvement of humans – to live longer and be more
productive: meditate, pop vitamin pills, get blood infusions or get
implants – continually advancing solutions emerging from the bio-tech
and medical industrial apparatus. But, as we already discovered in the
context of the lean startup, the beneficiaries of such processes are not
necessarily the consumers, users or those experimented upon, but those
whose ideas of societal, biological, ecological or political 'improvement'
are thereby furthered. We are in the middle of these changes and we
struggle for critical distance. What seems to be clear is that these new
technologies are now part of our environment (see McLuhan, 1964) and
that entrepreneurship plays an important role in deciding which of the
new possibilities arising will come to be realised and how this will
change the ways we live and work.

4

Entrepreneurship as Seeing With New Eyes

▰▰▰ world-making

In our final chapter, we turn to views that develop intricate ideas and openings that avoid binary segregation of creation and destruction, and with this, we return to our initial suggestion that phenomenology offers some rather intriguing insights for entrepreneurship. We want to start with a remarkable book by Charles Spinosa, Fernando Flores and Hubert Dreyfus (1997). The authors suggest an understanding of entrepreneurship that is both specific and inclusive. They call it 'disclosing new worlds', which, we will see, is plentiful, multiple and imaginative. It paints a stark contrast to the notion of the heroic entrepreneur who somehow knows something no one else does – a great idea turned opportunity. Spinosa and colleagues (1997) describe a subtle process that begins with people being part of their world. We are all immersed and attuned to the hustle and bustle around us; we barely notice the floor on which we walk or the facades we pass; we are habituated into social mores, taken in by fashions, trends and by ways of doing and saying things that chime, quite naturally, with our social roles and identities. These give us purpose and aims, and they help select which rules apply when we undertake our respective projects and tasks through which we continually, step by step, reproduce our existence. In other words, we are not creatures who look at the world in constant puzzlement, but we dwell in a lived-in world where, for the most part, we take explicit notice of things only when something goes wrong, is missing or gets in the way of us doing what we ought to do.

It is worth pausing here for a moment to appreciate just how different this way of thinking is. We don't start with a scientific view of the world, where everything is constantly evaluated, dissected or made subject to critical enquiry. We start from within the familiar, within which we are situated as whole beings, minds and bodies, entangled and interacting with other humans, animals, plants, soil, buildings and everything else, without having to think that much about each item in isolation. This suggests that we somehow already 'know' something about others and the otherness around us. At least, we know how to handily use objects and tools, how to cross a road in traffic and how to behave in a workplace or classroom, even if we may not ever have thought about this in detail. We would most likely struggle saying exactly how we do so because everything is just too familiar. Spinosa and colleagues call this a 'style'. Style brings all these various practices and materials together so much so that we can consider ourselves, who we are and how we do things, as being grounded (or, more specifically, constituted) in a style. Style refers to the common, habituated, engrained and unthought ways of acting, thinking and being, and it is the equivalent to our world. When style changes, we come to experience a new world in which the things around us are different; we engage with them in altered ways; and as a result, we are different kinds of people. Spinosa and colleagues therefore call moments in which 'style' changes the 'disclosure of a new world'. And this is precisely where Spinosa and colleagues get quite clever because they suggest that we should reserve the term 'entrepreneurship' for those acts that are involved in the disclosure of new worlds. Entrepreneurship, then, would be quite specifically concerned with creating new styles, with making new worlds.

As this is all a little abstract and densely philosophical, it is helpful to work through a few examples. The first one, provided by Spinosa and colleagues, is both illuminating and somewhat disappointing: King C. Gillette's eponymously branded disposable razor. Such an item would have been unthinkable in a world (a style) marked by craft, where items were handmade and expensive, and where people were attuned to the appreciation of longevity and the inheritance of goods between generations, while engaging in practices of caring, repairing and mending. But with mass production and the cheap availability of steel and later plastic arises the possibility of a new style where we buy throwaway products, purchase new things because continuous consumption signals our status to others, alleviates our boredom, or where 'shopping' gives us an affective buzz (see Reckwitz, 2017). Gillette's entrepreneurial contribution was to take part in the facilitation of this shift. He *sensed* the coming age of a throwaway society before others had caught on to it. This is important: it was not an opportunity out there, but a way of making new ways of living possible by *articulating* that new style. This involves questioning the old and explaining the new, creating difference and distinction in a way that old traditions and practices may be refined or extended. Entrepreneurship as world-making is both sensitive to anomalies and willing to bend or break the rules of the game, and it is eloquent and persuasive in making others join in the creation of a new disclosive space, which then needs to be expanded through *cross-appropriation* and *reconfiguration*.

The razor example is well chosen because it shows at once how entrepreneurs can be part of the disclosing of new ways of living but – and this is the disappointing bit – such new styles need not be ethical, nor does progress have to be 'positive'. But they can be. This is shown by a second example in form of Chris Steyaert's (2014) reading of what happens in the movie *The Full Monty*. It is set in the late 1990s in Sheffield, UK, a city hit hard by industrial decline, rampant levels of unemployment, poverty and hopelessness. It details how a group of unemployed steelworkers struggling with their families and friends, and with social expectations and cultural norms, try to make some money by forming a male striptease act. Most of all, they struggle with themselves, so that the change of style means not just that new routines (and they get quite good at these) and practices become possible but that their identities change. We witness how friendships and family ties are forged, broken and mended, and how all of this is quite an embarrassing, desperate, existential, challenging and transformative effort. What is so nice about Steyaert's beautiful interpretation of these changes is how the new style is not in opposition to the old; it is not disruptive; nor is it an experiment, with risk mitigated through controlled bet sizes. Instead, we find lots of humour and tender care, as well as anger and doubt. What is entrepreneurial here is what Hjorth and Steyaert (2021) elsewhere call the quality of stirring and disturbing. It is a provocation that first requires the capacity to be affected by others. In this way, entrepreneurship is political: 'a process driven by the urge for equality, and is entrepreneurial to the extent that it creates organization in its pursuit of new possibilities for living for hitherto missing people' (Hjorth & Steyaert, 2021: 257). This also brings us back to Grayson Perry, with whom we began, and whose journey we can read in similar fashion – art as way of developing a style that expresses who and what you are. Only now, once a new style has emerged, can we all imagine and readily discuss the opportunities of making it in art, being working class, being a potter, while liking shiny PVC or pretty dresses, a style that was in need of being made actual by creative activity (Hjorth, Holt & Steyaert, 2015: 603).

Here we also find a reconsideration of entrepreneurship beyond the commercially driven example of the disposable razor, which is marked by a new style that heightens economic gain while externalities pile up, literally, in the form of heaps of waste, and also beyond the notion of social enterprises, which often come in to fix holes in the system, without revising the system itself. Instead, we find a different kind of experimentation where the figure of the entrepreneur, their identities, bodies and relations with those around them are experimented on, each step a loosening, allowing for an opening towards something new that may or may not settle in subsequent steps. Once more Spinosa et al.'s (1997) careful outline of the ways new worlds form and transform those who live in them points to an unsettling, stirring, disharmonious sense of no longer belonging, like the steelworkers in *The Full Monty* who no longer feel at home in their mothballed steel mills, nor in the masculine identities that had, for generations, been forged and hardened in them. Holding on to disharmony means becoming not-at home, an uncanny beginning from out of which alternative lines of flight may be experimentally taken. Here we can also glance at a more nuanced understanding of Nietzsche's 'will to power', one which begins with being affected, bodily, and when we are then '… in full possession of a power to act, what Nietzsche calls affirmative "will to power," we connect with active forces' which increase our capacity to be open and to affirm creation, rather than passive forces, associated with control and acceptance of the status quo (Hjorth, 2014: 54). With this, we also enter a different idiom of process, flow and becoming (Tsoukas & Chia, 2002) in which the things of the world are not isolated, timeless and clearly bounded objects but one which affirms duration, repetition, difference and divergence. Like an infinite cloth that is being continually woven, the new may continue the patterns of the old but in the process of weaving, there is also always the chance for things to come together differently. Massumi (in Hjorth, 2014: 54) calls this the 'virtual', a 'seeping edge', the very moment radical openness of the future 'leaks' into reality, where the potential for difference lies. To explore the role of entrepreneurship in this creative advance of the universe, we turn to the notion of the virtual.

the virtual

We are now in a position to develop further Reckwitz's outline of three types of novelty *(I, II, III)*: the first, we recall, was radical disruption; the second piecemeal but ongoing progress; and the third revolved around the affective buzz from the new without requiring either disruptive or progressive qualities. Via Spinosa and colleagues we have seen something different emerge, which combines affect with a sense of progression, and while this creates a new world it does not need to be disruptive. How is this possible? It is helpful here to turn to a couple of papers by Munro (2018) and Hjorth and Johannisson (2008) who ask us to conceive of the new, and of creativity, in terms of curiosity and the question 'what if'. What they are after, similar to Steyaert and Spinosa and colleagues, is openness to novelty which neither just revamps the old, nor does it merely copy what it sees elsewhere. For this, they draw an interesting distinction between the *possible*, the *potential* and the *virtual*. The *possible* is what we can see from already existing things: we can see that it is possible to produce cheap consumer goods, as there are many successful examples such as Gillette's razor. The *possible* can be extrapolated from the past – its orientation is historical. The *potential*, on the other hand, focusses on the present, taking its cue from what is already visible or noticeable, such as using social media to drive business, rather than relying on point of sales marketing or traditional advertising. Neither the 'possible' nor the 'potential' orient themselves towards the future. This is the realm of the 'virtual', which is something that is not yet a 'thing' at all but rather in the process of becoming something; it has to do with being affected, and with curiosity – with the question *'what if'*.

Let us explore this through an example. Achilles Mbebe (2021) imagines how African countries can create genuinely different trajectories from those taken by Western developed countries, which also do not just perpetuate the status quo. Mbebe (2020) refers to this as *Afropolitanism*: a cultural, historic and aesthetic sensibility that unites a plurality of African cultures in one geographical space (Balakrishnan, 2017). Mbebe begins by pointing out the radically different characteristics of states, religion, community, culture and personal experiences, skills and movement patterns in many African regions, which have all become mingled in what he calls an extreme fragmentation (Mbebe, 2020: 238), patchworks of spheres that emerged in many post-colonial economies and societies:

> … a diffracted economy, comprising various, more or less intertwined, sometimes parallel, regional nodes that maintained changing and extremely volatile relations with international economic networks. A multiplicity of economic territories, often within the same country, sometimes nested within one another and often disjointed, is emerging out of this extreme fragmentation.

These are not clear-cut economies or nations, neatly organised by industry codes, and boundaries fencing in linguistically and culturally homogeneous cultures. They are layered and multiple; they do not abide by fixed demarcations apart, perhaps, from being interspersed by regions in which oils, minerals or diamonds are extracted, which operate in their own exploitative regimes. Add to this the vast distances and the effects of migration, war and state formation and disintegration, the radical alterations of technology, in particular the smartphone, the shifting roles of gender and selfhood and much more. We may read Mbebe's efforts at establishing the notion of Afropolitanism as an entrepreneurial venture: the development of a poetic and creative space of African futures as emerging out of the shadows – and against the fading structures of colonialism. Mbebe (2020: 60) calls Afropolitanism: *'an aesthetics that can say something new and meaningful to the world in general'*, where something quintessentially African can be sensed, as a kind of transformation (not repetition of the old, not copying of what others do) that takes place.

Now let us return to the idea of the virtual. The philosopher Brian Massumi provides an example of what he calls a 'topological figure':

> A topological figure is defined as the continuous transformation of one geometrical figure into another. Imagine a pliable coffee cup. Join the surfaces of the brim, enlarge the hole in the handle, and then stretch it so that all its sides are equally thick. You get a doughnut. You could then tie this doughnut into complex knots. All of the geometrical figures you can create in this way are versions of the same topological figure. (Massumi, 2002: 134)

So here is the trick. What Mbebe asks us to do is not akin to taking an old coffee cup as a prototype for any future objects, repeating long-established ways in which its walls can hold liquid, or the handle allows for the insertion of fingers. Nor does he suggest we look around at how ceramic cups are everywhere replaced by plastic containers. Instead, he wants us to take the cup merely as one possible form, which can be twisted and stretched into virtually any other form within the material constraints of the given object. This does therefore not mean that everything is possible: the cup cannot be turned into a car or a bike, but within the limits of its topological form, there are endless creative possibilities to explore. Some of these forms will be familiar either because they have been around a long time (the coffee cup or the doughnut as 'possible' forms) or because they correspond as *potential* with what we see around us now (perhaps resembling the streamlined contours of electric vehicles). But some will be different and new, so much so, that they require what Spinosa et al. have outlined in terms of *sensing, articulating, cross-appropriating* and *reconfiguring*. It is this capacity to hold on to fluid, unsettled forms that Mbebe translates into the virtual capacity of:

> ... people who can express themselves in more than one language. They are developing, sometimes without their knowing it, a transnational culture which I call "Afropolitan" culture.

Notice the difference from the ways in which much traditional entrepreneurship research characterises the entrepreneur: risk-seeking, being decisive, calculative or experimental – or exhibiting almost super(hu) man skills and traits. Mbebe's entrepreneurs, by contrast, are those who have, by choice or necessity, moved around and been thrown into contexts where they learned multiple languages and ways of expression and thinking. The point is not whether they are good at a few things in particular, instead it is about being good at connecting, relating, dealing with others and coping with change and difference – and they are at home in this agility, fluidity and multiplicity, which bestows them a creative openness that may just help birth Afropolitanism as a new style. With this we can return to our earlier question: why is so much stuff out there not new at all? – which Reckwitz answers with the affective charging of sameness. We can now further qualify this because it is often a case of the *possible* – a return to the past – or the *potential* – what can be imagined based on what is currently the case. With the notion of the virtual, Hjorth and others are trying to carve out a space for the new that breaks with the emulation of past and present, and to focus on the future. Perhaps, and here is where Mbebe's book ends, this harbours the possibility of an African future that not merely repeats the destructive cycles of capitalism that the developed world has written into history, but the possibility of a genuinely new world (this time following an Afropolitan style) in which the agglomeration of wealth, knowledge and information and of means of production is replaced by more organic ways of living.

What we see as entrepreneurial here is what Hjorth et al. (2015: 605) describe as '... the already more that spills over (what comes next) into particular arrangements and orders'. This is a temporal space in which the virtual 'leaks' into the actual; a difference in the advance of things that has not yet settled into habit, routine and thus bureaucracy, management and control, but is in the making, in the process of formation and organisation. The entrepreneur abets this process by which the proto-organisational forms of *what ifs* are brought into being; they direct 'the world's nextness' (Hjorth et al., 2015: 605).

blandness

Tracing this proto-organising, emerging and informing quality of entrepreneurship further, we are invited to look for ideas outside the prism of Western logic, and with outcomes beyond profit-seeking or market control, instead emphasising resistance, emancipation, or self-positioning (Woods, Dell & Carroll, 2022). One such idea emerges from François Jullien's (2004) work, a sinologist interested in ancient Chinese texts and practices relating to warfare, poetry and everyday life. Jullien makes a provocative claim: That blandness is the source of great potential, and it should therefore be cultivated and cherished. For most of us, blandness is a negative term. We despise bland food and bland conversations; pull our noses at bland dress senses; and are bored by bland landscapes. We look down at bland objects such as industrial containers or pallets which are just standardised square constructions with no real individual distinction – millions of these are ferried on ships, trains and lorries everyday around the world and they can be made with little effort or skill required. What we want is a distinction: the sharpness of chilli cutting through a dish, making the taste buds tingle; a star character in a film who stands out and whom we remember; or a landscape cleaved by a dramatic waterfall, whose wild stirrings arrest our eye, and which makes the rest of the scenery fade into the insignificant background. In business too, we want distinction: strategists tell us we have to be different and focus, avoiding at all cost to get stuck in the bland middle.

The problem with all of this is that distinction elevates a few criteria above all others and it neglects the success stories of the things that are not shiny and individual. These can be pretty amazing, like the pallets and containers which are the real success stories in the history of industrialisation and global trade. They are successful precisely because they are not special or individual, but allow for standardisation and interchange – they can be stacked and moved anywhere in the world, as their blandness and indistinction can be anticipated and worked with everywhere. We are here reminded of a little nonsense poem by Christian Morgenstern, retold by de Certeau (1988: 121), about a picket fence. Such fences are made up from wooden lattice nailed onto beams, so that there is a gap between each piece of wood. The space between the lattice is as much part of the fence as the wood itself, and the poem makes that its paradoxical focus:

An architect who saw this sight approached it suddenly one night, removed the spaces from the fence and built of them a residence.

Jullien wants to wean us off this fixation with the few criteria that stand out, arrest the eye, captivate our senses and reorient us towards the vast remainder, the rest, the leftover or background against which anything first can gain relief. Take fireworks – we are drawn in by the bright flashes and the shattering sounds of the explosions, so much so, that we forget the necessity of the blackness of the night sky to first make this spectacle possible. Imagine fireworks setting off in mid-day, under a gleaming sun or next to a metal factory with stomping presses and shrill light of welding machines fizzing through windows. We would barely notice the flares and the bangs of the explosions would merely melt into the busy soundscape of industrial machination. Without the silent blackness of the night, the fireworks would not be able to stand out. What we really notice, therefore, is neither the light nor the explosions but the difference between these and their backgrounds (Bateson, 1987: Ch. 4.9.4). We may say that what we see and hear is light breaking upon darkness and sound breaking upon silence. Only where there is dark can there be light; only with silence is noise possible. But that is not all. Jullien argues that not only do we need to consider opposites and extremes such as light/dark or silence/noise, but that it is possible to oppose these extreme distinctions with something else, something with lacks those distinctions: with the bland. Blandness is a condition in which neither light nor dark dominate; it is a washed out grey, the murky, boring, uninteresting, unrememberable and insignificant. It is the background to all distinctions, and therefore a source of infinite potential.

Jullien (2004) takes his cue from ancient Chinese landscape paintings. The painter Ni Zhan, for example, who painted similar landscapes throughout his life not, as Jullien argues, because he wanted to represent a particular geographical place, or perfect a specific motif, but to achieve a detachment from the motif. Over his life, Ni Zhan worked towards ever greater sparseness, attempting to paint a landscape that was a specific image but at the same time so generic that it could have been any other landscape as well. Here is how Jullien (2004: 37–39) describes one of these pictures:

The ink used to paint this landscape has been generously diluted. The range of colors is narrow, and pale overall. The strokes appear not so much in individually distinct traces as in marks meltingly submerged into forms. The painter has even refused to treat distant objects differently, as one usually does, by reducing the amount of detail or blurring the outlines. Near and far are fundamentally homogeneous, "reflecting each other," as it is commonly said, and becoming equals under the viewer's gaze. The gaze travels evenly from one edge of the scroll to the other; only the vertical lines of the delicate boughs tie together the two shores, keeping the various planes on the surface. No more impulsive brushstroke than these disturbs the calm that unfolds across the different parts of the scroll; no decorative, or merely pleasing, touch relieves the platitude of the whole. Yet, drained of all opacity – unburdened of all weightiness – as such a landscape is, it does not lack its own substance and in this differs from its all-too-numerous imitations. The sketched shapes possess volume, the spottiness of the sparse dots garbs the contours in a bit of moss, and a few darker strokes delineate more clearly, here and there, the edges of things. Nothing here strives to incite or seduce; nothing aims to fix the gaze or compel the attention. Yet this landscape exists fully as a landscape. The Chinese critics traditionally characterize this in one word: *dan,* the "bland."

Jullien also comments on how this artistic detachment from specific things was matched by Ni Zhan's biography. Born into a wealthy family, he left behind his possessions in his later life, wandering the country and riversides, sleeping in simple sheds or monasteries. With Nietzsche, we may detect an affirmative, open and creatively active process, influenced by being bodily affected. Over the course of his life, Ni Zhan's paintings became sparser and sparser; human life disappeared, and with it all detachment to things, forms and matter. Jullien (2004: 42) cites the Chinese philosopher Laozi (also known as Lao-Tze or Lao Tzu):

Music and things dear and delectable stop the passerby in his tracks.

When it passes through [that is, "comes out of"] the mouth, the Dao is insipid and flavorless: it cannot be perceived, it cannot be heard, but it is inexhaustible.

When we try to contrast this to the distinct, such as the sharpness of the chilli spice, the shrillness of a loud noise or the glare of a bright firework, we realise quickly how hard it is to speak of something that is, well, not really something but not nothing either. The qualities of the bland are undetectable, imperceptible, inaudible and unspeakable – but they are still almost something. It is like looking at a blurred picture, trying to find out what we see. Where a high-definition image may give us a clear sense of 'this is this or that', the blur requires us to do some work. We need to put in efforts of interpretation: Could it be this? Or maybe we see something at first and then we realise, no, it is not that at all and something else emerges. And if the picture is very blurred, we may never be quite sure – we may go back to it over and over again, trying to find out what we might find next. The blander the picture, the more it may surprise us, perhaps, that there is so much possibility here, inexhaustible numbers of forms and figures that can come to the fore over time. We have already come across the term virtuality – and Massumi's flat doughnut coffee cup – to indicate something beyond the potential and the possible: something creative, vague and not quite settled. Jullien gives us further artistic examples in the form of the bland landscape, and in his book, there are others ranging from poetry to music and food, each suggesting that there is much richness in blandness – not because it is obvious or clear, but because the bland can be so many things, whereas the rich or specific can only ever be what it is. This is what Jullien (2004: 42) says about the inexhaustible:

> ...the "inexhaustible" source of that which constantly unfolds without ever allowing itself to be reduced to a concrete manifestation or completely apprehended by the senses: that which transcends all particular actualisations and remains rich in virtuality.

Far from this being a purely artistic endeavour, Jullien elaborates on military strategies concerned with defending or deciding matters of statecraft. He contrasts the idea of the bland to the kind of warfare favoured by the ancient Greeks from whom we have inherited many contemporary ideas, including how to do entrepreneurial or corporate strategy. What counted for the Greeks was the display of courage (a form of virtue) in battle. Hand-to-hand combat was seen to be a fair and glorifying way of fighting, as was an open battle formation where clashes involved heavily armed and shielded warriors (hoplites) marching against the enemy in formal lines (phalanxes) without hesitation. Cheating or deceit was seen to be unbecoming as were forms of warfare that attacked the enemy from afar – the use of spears, arrows or javelins was all considered to be of lower virtue than fighting each other face to face (see Chia & Holt, 2009: 187).

While the block-shaped phalanx hits the enemy with concentrated force, the bland suggests a lack of impact upon reality, a kind of arti- and superficiality. So how does that make the bland effective (or rather efficacious)? Do the might and organised momentum released by impact with a phalanx-like formation not inherently disintegrate any opposition in the field? Well, perhaps, but what if 'the field' is not the only place of action? You may also think of the metaphor of the tree and the long strands of grass in a strong wind. The oak tree, like the phalanx, will confront the gusts, carve a clear distinction from the environment, and it will not buckle under strain until it reaches a point of breakage. Long strands of grass bend and twist in the wind. Offering no resistance and in so being 'bland', they can simply bend back up again once the storm is over, when the oak tree lies there broken. But we can push the idea of the bland even further: What if the enemy does not show up on the day of the battle, or if they are simply invisible, not dressed up as card-carrying warriors, but masquerading as citizens, farmers or peasants, perhaps those who serve or service an occupying force as local haircutters, cooks or mechanics, but who really then secretly cut throats, poison soups or sabotage vehicles? Here, the enemy is invisible, leaving the phalanx standing in the sun all day while causing havoc outside of the official hours of battle.

The ancient Greeks had a nice term for this – *metis* – which is the name of a Goddess and means 'cunning'. Cunning behaviour is interesting from an entrepreneurial perspective because it allows a weaker party to outwit a stronger one. Think of a small entrepreneurial outfit facing stiff competition from established firms. The entrepreneur can typically not compete on price, nor on variety offered. They may face legal challenges and they can't afford pricey lawyers. They may lose out on real estate, not being able to buy themselves into the high street. They have not got the same marketing budget; they will lose out on top staff who will get higher salaries and more benefits at a big firm; they lack the capacity to invest the same into product development and organisational structures; and so on and so forth. So how do small entrepreneurial outfits manage to emerge or survive next to these behemoths? One answer is to apply the distinction between force (what we have referred to as a distinctive, phalanx-like approach) and cunning. This means looking at aspects that may go in favour of the entrepreneur, which means not facing the bigger competitors heads on. What may that be? They may be able to offer levels of customisation by engaging with customers on a level that exceeds what a large company can do. We have to remind ourselves that the large company only works because it is able to systematise and routinise things. They work well because they can repeat things over and over again and for this they invest in bureaucratic structures and overheads, standardisation and repetitively broken-down steps and long-term planning. This logic has long been recognised, for example, by Adam Smith who, in the book *The Wealth of Nations*, shows how a small number of workers who distribute tasks can manufacture many times what the same number of workers can do when they make each item one at a time.

But understanding the bland shows us some of the vulnerabilities that come from being big. The whole setup of producing standardised things takes a long time; it takes a lot of investment (machines, training, developing processes, inventory, market testing and so on) and only when a firm manages to sell many, many items, is it able to 'break even' and reap the benefits of these large investments in time, effort and resources. Now compare this to the 'bland' entrepreneur who works with general machines and skills, able reprogramme or retool these for small batches; or imagine employees in smaller firms acquiring generalist skills to cover a wider spectrum of work. Large firms will use more specialised machines which can only make one thing at a time and they train people to operate the machines, or deal with customers or suppliers, by teaching them small repetitive movements often in specialised departments. Big firms are therefore often efficient but not flexible; their strength of being able to pump out wares at great volumes becomes a weakness in an environment where rapid and constant adjustment and customisation is favoured.

flow, presence and absence

But it is not just a matter of being nimbler. We can connect the discussion of blandness more directly with the virtual and with Spinosa et al.'s notion of world-making. As we have seen, big organisations tend to have certain ways of looking at the world, which are grounded in standardised methods, relying on abstraction, often using quantitatively generated data, which are channelled through bureaucratic processes. They may conduct consumer research and look at factory outputs or failure rates in datasets that are already created automatically, and which code and therefore replace the need to go anywhere in person to find out about each individual issue. Whenever processes of data collection and analysis to support a big firm are standardised and routinised, they become efficient ways of looking at the whole operation without getting bogged down in time-consuming detail. Large firms often employ computing technologies for such things: enterprise resource planning systems, for example, map the entirety of firm operations, calculating continually how things are (stock levels, orders, machine capacities, workload planning, etc.) as well as analysing whether interventions are needed (profitability, failure rates, sick days taken, etc.). Using big data approaches, more recent applications no longer ask managers to monitor things all the time and make many decisions throughout the day, and instead make decisions themselves, based on historical data coupled with machine learning algorithms. But there are a few curious things happening here. Such calculation inherently remains partial and therefore limited. Despite such analyses comprising vast amounts of data, there is always a remainder or rest that escapes calculation, the other side of distinctions that we encountered above as the bland. And even though computers calculate almost in real time, they can never catch up with a world that moves on, re-entering these very calculations into its advance.

We want to make one more step in qualifying such blandness, not just in terms of its indistinction, but also in its flowing, unsettled character, which Mbebe identifies in highly fragmented groups, and which Spinoza et al. indicate in terms of an unhomely, uncanny, disharmonic quality humming below the seemingly rhythmic patterns of organised life. Here we may invoke the pre-Socratic philosopher Heraclitus, who lived some 2,500 years ago, and who left behind little more than a few fragments of his ideas. One of these states: 'all things flow'. Another one is that you 'can't step into the same river twice'. The Greek word for river – or rather for stream – is *rhei* and it is associated with the figure of Proteus, a sea god and shepherd of the bodies in the oceans (in particular seals). We find Proteus in our current use of the word '*protean*', which indicates flexibility, adaptability and versatility, and we even find the word *rhei* turning into *rhe*ology, the study of movement and transformation. Proteus comes to us via Homer's Odyssey, where he is depicted as a 'slippery character because he can change his shape at will' (Wilson, 2018: 50). Proteus is as fluid as the water he stands for: he can metamorphose into different forms: '... he will change shape to every animal on earth, and then water and holy fire' (Wilson, 2018: line 415). A protean coffee cup would make Brian Massumi very happy. This idea of protean metamorphosis has been taken up widely in art too. The artist Cy Twombly, for example, painted Proteus's transformation from 'a lion with a mane, then snake, then leopard, then a mighty boar, then flowing water, then a leafy tree' (Wilson, 2018, line 455). But if you look up this picture,[1] you will see that Twombly does not paint anything that looks like a sea god, a lion, a snake, a leopard, a boar or even anything that resembles flowing water; perhaps we can just make out some kind of tree, but that is all. All there is is paint (Staff, 2017: 44). It is as if he painted not so much the specific forms (the lion which becomes the snake and so on) but the in-between, that bit that is always in the latent spaces or interstices between any of the forms. This is also the bland, neither this nor that and yet everything all at once, the lion turning into snake turning into leopard and so on. Twombly, in a way, has painted the spaces from the fence, not the posts or lattice.

Another example is Kwementyaye "Kathleen" Petyarre's painting: Mountain Devil Lizard Dreaming (After Sandstorm; Kathleen Petyarre, 1996).[2] This lizard exists and, like a chameleon, it changes its colours in response to threat, and it can freeze its movements entirely (Groz, 2008: 94). But just like Twombly, Petyarre does not depict the lizard in any discernible shape – there is no attempt at representing the creature. Instead, the paint becomes the lizard – it is in the making, it shows itself in and as a shape shifter. Here, everything belongs together in an 'open whole' (Kohn, 2013): the skin, the territory, the people dwelling in and alongside fauna and flora, and alongside myths (the lizard as an ancestral being existing in a reality beyond the mundane) and dreams. To try and be in this landscape without drawing boundaries or singling out this or that object so that it can be assessed, measured and put to use is a way of preserving the complexity of the world.

For us, Petyarre and Twombly's examples are fascinating because they manage to stay in the flow, in the inexhaustible and bland, and yet they still manage to produce something actual from out of this: a real painting you can look at. Being artists, they are happy to stop here: letting what emerges depend on the co-construction of meaning between the picture and someone looking at it. They express this shifting kaleidoscope of perception without privileging one appearance over another (e.g., the landscape on a sunny day being more important or real than the washed out, barely visible one in the midst of a storm), but let the things emerge in their fluidity – in their changing characteristics. In contrast, we see the role of entrepreneurship as going one step further by turning such inexhaustible potential into specific, concrete and limited actualities.

new eyes

Here we have to inject a caveat. Of course, this does not mean that for entrepreneurs, all the time, everything should look like Twombly or Petyarre's paintings, nor should we try to build houses from gaps. We would have no grasp of the world, nothing to hold on to, nothing we could name with language, and so we would have no science, no abstraction and so on. We still need the forms of the lion and the snake, and we also need names for these processes – metamorphosis for example – and we label the story a myth and so on – but a certain danger encroaches when we give all these solid forms too much credence. Following Spinosa et al., 1997, as well as Gartner (2008), entrepreneurs facilitate that process of meaning-making and keep going until routines are beginning to settle, and new ways of thinking, talking and being become accepted. Then entrepreneurship is done and management can take over (Hjorth, 2014).

What Proteus teaches us through the myth of the shapeshifting god, who is all these things at different times, is that we too are always shifting. We are reminded of the riddle of the Sphinx: what walks on four legs, then on two, then on three? That is of course the human being – crawling as a baby, then walking on both legs, then using a walking stick as a third leg, before, presumably, crawling again. We look around ourselves and see the same pattern: to see a tree is to take one form out from the flow from seed to becoming a pile of logs, then hummus or ash. A stone – much slower of course – is in-between being dust, and then a rock, and then a brick wall and then dust again. All things change over time, sometimes faster and sometimes slower. If we pay attention, we may notice how the world around us changes and how we change, too. We may remember 'this tree', or 'this person', or 'this organisation' – and then we are really surprised when 'that tree' suddenly has grown; or when 'this person' turns out to be not nice at all, or when 'this organization', maybe one with lots of shiny products which we have adored for so long and spent so much money on, now turns out to be environmentally disastrous, or employs slave labour, or otherwise had you fooled all the time. Or imagine being in business and thinking that this here is your customer segment, or this here is your industry – only to find out that things could be very different, that we only saw one of the many versions of what things can be, not their entirety. We can never see all things. We cannot see the seed, the tree and the humus the tree turns into all at once – this means that our current view, right now, just showing the tree in one instance of its journey, should not be privileged over all others. What we need, in a way, are many different eyes for looking at the world. This is, more or less, the point the philosopher Merleau-Ponty (1964/1993) makes in a famous essay called 'Eye and mind', where he says:

> Scientific thinking, a thinking which looks on from above, and thinks of the object-in-general, must return to the "there is" which precedes it; to the site, the soil of the sensible and humanly modified world such as it is in our lives and for our bodies – not that possible body which we may legitimately think of as an information machine but this actual body I call mine, this sentinel standing quietly at the command of my words and my acts.

Before we begin to abstract, before we find out that there is this 'thing' and that 'thing', each having particular properties which can be used for some purpose or other, we need to return to the 'there is'. Merleau-Ponty is one of the best-known proponents of 'phenomenology' which, as we have suggested, is concerned with a return to things as they are (or as they appear) rather than with abstractions or essences. It involves attempting to describe that world as precisely as possible in the way in which human beings experience it. This return to what is 'just there' is not an unscientific way of looking – or rather it is not 'just' a layperson's view – but a completely legitimate way of understanding the world. And not just that, being fundamental to seeing new things it involves paying attention to metamorphoses: the landscape changes, and you, the observer, change too.

Nothing is the same once you have taken even the smallest of steps. This is what Heraclitus indicates when saying that one cannot step in the same river twice: All things flow. But it's even better than that. This leaves us free to forget the abstract characteristics that we inherently, automatically and pre-perceptually attach to the things we encounter and to try and see things as they appear to us – we can do so over and over again and each time we can see new things. Let us tune in to how a phenomenologist talks about experiencing landscapes:

> [A] landscape is not a physical constant that is simply given to empirical observation, description and measurement. It is rather given only in relation to its inhabitants, to their lives, movements and purposes, and the places where they dwell, and draws its meanings from these relations. Thus people and landscape – to recycle an overused anthropological formula – are 'mutually constituted'. Landscapes take on meanings and appearances in relation to people, and people develop skills, knowledge and identities in relation to the landscapes in which they find themselves. (Ingold, 2011: 129)

A landscape is therefore not a fixed thing, out there, which we can investigate like a scientist tries to dissect some specimen in an experimental setting. If we try to follow the phenomenologists, we want to find out how the landscape appears to us. It is worth taking it slowly here and work out that difference. It is not a matter of what something 'is' – this landscape here is lush, or green, or built up. This chair here is square, has three legs and is made from wood. All these are abstract qualities that could be written down in a ledger which can be read in order to create a general, agreed set of ideas about the 'thing' in question.

Moving away from the abstract we no longer have a 'landscape' or a 'chair' in isolation, but what we look at is couplets such as 'observer+landscape' or 'observer+chair'. The person to whom the thing appears is now part of the equation. This means that it matters how we feel, where we are, how we look, what time of day, what weather and how our moods are – all these affect how we see. To experience a landscape on a misty day is not just a matter of seeing less (less colour, less detail, just greyscales, etc.). The difference, Tilley (1994: 12) suggests, is not in the landscape but in the way the landscape is *perceived*. Going back to our little formula, it is now located in the '+' that connects 'observer+landscape': a misty landscape is not the same colourful and vibrant landscape which is just greyed out at the moment, but it is an entirely new perception, a new appearance, which brings different sensory impressions and different possibilities.

This now brings us back to artists such as Twombly and Petyarre, who try to express this shifting kaleidoscope of perception without privileging one appearance over another (e.g., the landscape on a sunny day being more important or real than the washed out, barely visible one in the midst of a storm), but let the things emerge in their fluidity – in their changing characteristics:

> The body is continually improvising its relationship with things precisely because it is not a closed mechanical system but constantly opening out itself to the world as it moves in it. The manner in which we sense the world remains forever incomplete and ambiguous because we always experience things from a particular point of view or relationship. (Tilley, 2004: 10)

What the phenomenologists want us to do is therefore to unlearn our abstract ways of seeing; be a little less clever thinking 'oh, I know what that is', and instead explore and be surprised – let ourselves marvel at things in a state of wonder about what there actually is.

Let us therefore attempt one last example by looking at one of the few artists who have written specifically about how art works. This is Paul Klee (1879–1940), a Swiss-born, German painter, poet and teacher of art, associated with the famous Bauhaus School. Klee's biography is important because it gives us clues about why he was concerned with overcoming old styles. He lived through tremendous historical changes, comprising the two World Wars, massive transformations brought by technology, where ways of working and living with cities and machines began taking over from manual rural life. Klee was affected: when the world makes no sense anymore, why should art? Out went picturesque representations and naturalism, and even those tropes that emphasised the ways in which humans experienced the world, such as impressionism, had become mute in the face of the terrors of machine-driven war fortresses that had laid waste to so many parts of the world. What was needed, in other words, was a new language for a truly modern world, and who but artists could purvey such ideas (Temkin, 1987: 13). The new came via playful and sometimes radical approaches, ranging from the nonsensical to the abstract.

But how does the artist create the abstract from the real? Klee enlists the example of a tree. There is a resemblance between the twisting network of its roots and its crown, yet both are entirely different. Klee likens the artist to the tree stem, drawing moisture from the roots and delivering sap to the ramified branches that make up its crown. The stem, like the artist, is a conduit that helps transform the real (or earthen) into the abstract (or aerial). When painting, Klee (1956: 19) asks us not start with a fully formed idea, but with nothing. Chaos. The infinite bleakness of an empty canvas. Then he asks us to draw a dot. That's all to begin with – the dot is not nothing but not really much of something either – an 'infinitely tiny elemental plane' or a timeless dead point, as he calls it. But now we have a start. From here we can start a line which is a tension between this point and another. And once we have a line, we can extend it so that we have plane, and then extend it further into a box or a circle. Lines, planes and spaces are charged with energy and they flow and connect like the sap moving through the tree. The point is that Klee reminds us of basic things: that painting (as well as looking at a painting) is about movement, bit by bit, which takes time. Over time many choices have to be made: straight or wobbly lines, extend this way or that way and so on. We move forward (extending the line) and stop to look (we 'catch our breath') and reflect (a counter-movement). We move on, encountering various other things: boats (wavy line), bridges (curved lines), a friendly person (converging line), and gradually realising their differences (separate lines), and so on. Creation is movement. Each new movement changes not just the emerging form but also the overall picture. This is why the artists stops and walks away, looking at the whole, before continuing.

This taking in of the whole 'undivided shape' of the object is the essence of creativity:

> Each choice is equally crucial for further progress. The choice would be easy if we could command an aerial view of the entire network of nodal points and radiating pathways still lying ahead. This is never the case. If we could map out the entire way ahead, no further search would be needed. As it is, the creative thinker has to make a decision about [their] route without having the full information needed for [their] choice. (Ehrenzweig, 1971: 37)

Klee's lines do not represent something already existing, but they produce what is visible. There is a childlike innocence at play here, one that is not restricted to painting definite forms (or *Gestalten*), but one which keeps the specific and the general together:

> The creative thinker has to advance on a broad front keeping open many options. [They] must gain a comprehensive view of the entire structure of the way ahead without being able to focus on any single possibility. (Ehrenzweig, 1971: 36)

The two quotes above are from a brilliant book by art historian Anton Ehrenzweig, who suggests this multi-dimensional way of looking at the whole picture is something children do but then lose when they are taught to paint in ways that resemble objects, thus becoming ashamed of their earlier doodles. We may therefore think of artists as needing to unlearn this learning and get back to the childlike innocence of seeing and drawing. We bring in Klee here because he gives us a few tricks with which we can regain at least some of this whole-picture seeing. He says:

> In painting, 'the picture' should be regarded as the object. The picture is the whole; the parts should be evaluated in relation to the whole, that is, in relation to the picture. (Klee, 1956: 47)

So let's try it out. We want to follow Klee (1976: 47) and draw a picture of a bird (Figure 4.1) but we don't start there. We start with the whole canvas. That is, for now, our whole. Then we draw a bird and we see its body composed of various parts. But we also notice the not-bird-space which is everything but the bird. We can also group this not-bird-space into corners and areas that make up the outer and inner limits of space. The artist can consider the relation to space and boundaries, how the parts constitute the 'thing', how that 'thing' relates to other 'things' and how to position all this for a viewer. Emphasising different spatial dimensions creates the illusion of depth, of before and front, and of volume and this kind of thinking.

We can try to translate that to entrepreneurship. An initial business idea or sense of opportunity may resemble a first dot. But that is not yet anything living for it takes time to stretch this dot into forms that are alive. The entrepreneur may ask if the dot is flexible enough to stretch into any shape and, if so, how to move on. Each step is a new beginning, a new set of choices because whatever is there is only one tiny, partial possibility next to all that which is thereby excluded. And so, like Klee's movements, the entrepreneur may stop to catch their breath, and reflect in a counter-movement where to relate what they have just created back to the whole. This makes entrepreneurship a process of being immersed within environments that present possibilities but also doubts. Here, the entrepreneur is not like a scientist who stands objectively isolated from the things they study, nor do they know in advance what their destination may be. Their journey is an ongoing, open, changing experiential movement (Zundel, 2012). Being 'in-the-world' means drawing lines and images, or like Grayson Perry, it means coiling vases into shapes. These are ways of life because they make the maker who they are. These experiences may involve a 'conflict between belief and belief' – there is no certainty, only 'questionable possibilities' (Schuetz, 1951: 171–172); different trajectories might unfold and unexpected change might occur, leading to uncertainty becoming visible, but each new movement is part of the way the whole

Figure 4.1 Wholes, parts, forms and edges.

universe changes and it requires counter-movements and pauses to catch one's breath (but where one is still in the movement, in the world) for questions of choices (extending a line or erasing it) can emerge.

Grayson Perry, the potter who we earlier identified as an entrepreneur, made a few dots to start with: performance art, film-making and pottery, and it was the latter that could be stretched out. And then he makes pots and vases that look almost as if they could be 'for sale at a country craft fair or in the homeware section of a department store' (Klein, 2009: 9). Here we notice echoes to the virtual we discussed earlier – it is not that the 'new' comes to Perry from outside of the world but we see a twisting of the material–form complex into something new by adorning them with funny, sexually explicit, deviant, critical or humourous images and texts, just like Klee's tree trunk transforms the roots into the crown. We may say, with Klee, that a pot or vase is not the full picture, which only arises once we put these objects in relation to the not-pot or not-vase: with the usual understanding of art, which excludes craft, decoration and domesticity, seeing them as lesser, more readily consumable commodities. In the bird-form language Klee has given us, the vase or pot is just one part of the picture as a whole. Or, similarly (this time borrowing from the philosopher Heidegger), we might say that the object consists not just of the clay, the form and the decoration, but also of its *purpose*, being a work of art and not a vessel in which to park flowers.

Another example from earlier is the toy store(y) owners. Imagine watching them grow their business and thinking: now that opportunity is like one big bird they caught here. Surely, there is nothing left for us to do – the market is full, their shiny store, now stocked high with shiny toys, is all there is to this town and we may as well not bother being entrepreneurs at all. But looking at this example through Klee's eyes, we might ask, 'What does this business stand in relation to? Is it the town or a particular group of customers; is it a specific idea of commerce or a narrow sense of child play?' Or we might ask, 'Why are we so obsessed looking at this big store/bird, and we forget that there is a whole lot of space round, which is also always already there?' We might ask, 'What about those bits that are overlooked (a technical terminology, borrowing from Law (2004), is to speak of the "manifestly absent" or "othered"): what alternatives to buying toys may exist in adult/child relations; which income groups want to spend more or less and are thus not served; what about practices that do not rely on disposable toys but instead support sustainable purchasing habits; and so on'. Klee does this in his paintings: The space around the thing (be that the 'opportunity' or the 'organisation or firm') is equally as interesting as the thing itself. And what about the space we have assumed to exist? Are we limited by the frame and who defines its boundaries and whether we have to stick to it? The painter Howard Hodgkin famously ignored that a painting 'ought' to stop where the canvas ends and drew the brush over the wooden frames. It's surprising how much changes when we question frames and borders, and when we change what is focus and background. The entrepreneur may also ask themselves: now I have a good sense of what my firm/ opportunity is, but does that mean I now neglect all the space around this? Is there not always an imbalance in the things we can see or do next to all the myriad, infinite things we do not see or do? Here lies some interesting potential, a potential that does not stem from a clear vision or neatly demarcated opportunity, plan or design. Instead, it is a flexibility that comes from being nimble and light-footed; moving and counter-moving; able to spin on our heels when we have to change things around; and not obsessed with one thing (a bird, for example) but able to see that any such 'thing' is in fact always connected to (and made up of) lots and lots of more stuff – the parts, the feathers, the flock, the canvas, boundaries, the absence around and so on.

notes

1. https://www.wikiart.org/en/cy-twombly/proteus
2. https://www.wikiart.org/en/kathleen-petyarre/mountain-devil-liz-ard-dreaming-after-sandstorm-1996

Final Thoughts

We began with the aim of addressing the reader directly, rather than sitting on the fence, so to speak, attempting a balanced review of entrepreneurship studies. Instead, we talked about entrepreneurship with a phenomenological interest. We feel that phenomenological thinking helps, because it turns us away from abstract questions such as: what are opportunities, to how an opportunity appears to someone, at some point in time. This replaces attempts of objectively settling things with a more subjective sensibility for how one comes to notice, what can be noticed and how different faculties of body and mind, as well as social relations, and all manner of apparatuses are involved in this. What we need to understand is how entrepreneurs come to notice possibilities for change in the world and how this change is created. This makes us question how entrepreneurs come to know anything in the first place; how they notice some things and not others; and how their noticing emerges from and shapes the ways they – and those around them – live in a world in which they (as well as us) were brought up and socialised, and to which degree they are able to reflect on the familiar things around them. Entrepreneurship involves changes in noticing which, in turn, are also changes in ways of being; it is a fringe work that weaves the fabric of life as a play of existing and new patterns. For entrepreneurship to facilitate this continuous creative advance, it can neither be subsumed by the regularising and controlling characteristics of management nor can it leave the work of interpreting different ways of seeing and being to an audience. Instead, it has to tend to the process of forming and in-forming that transforms given contexts, injecting a degree of plasticity into them so that they can be re-moulded to let new forms emerge.

Much in the entrepreneurship literature, including Schumpeter's creativity and Kirzner's alertness, already suggests that entrepreneurs have an intimacy with the development of the new, which neither just emerges from nothing nor is it just an advance of the old. We drew on phenomenology and, in turn, on artistic approaches, to try and develop ideas on how newness can be brought out by those who dwell in a world that is so familiar to them that what may be different, strange or new needs an act of disclosure that arrives without conceptual clarity, clear boundaries or labels but announces itself by way of irritation, unsettledness or perplexion. Entrepreneurship entails a sensitivity towards such phenomena, and in acting upon them, entrepreneurs help birth the new into the world. This often includes collective efforts of utilising and building infrastructures, social spaces, communities and imaginaries, as well as concrete organisational practices (Holm & Beyes, 2022).

Thinking about entrepreneurship in terms of multiplicities is a phenomenological move, as it suggests that appearances can be different and as there is nothing but appearance, we have an influence on how things come to matter to us. This means that what we experience as the world around us is only one way of how things come together, and matters could always be different. Entrepreneurship is that mixing and stirring movement that dislodges sedimented and encrusted patterns. Hannah Arendt (1958) draws on the notion of 'natality', 'the new beginning inherent in birth [that] can make itself felt in the world only because the newcomer possesses the capacity of beginning something anew'. Note the opening up here; it is not a destruction of the old, but the joining of new generations into existing ones. It is what she calls an insertion of 'plurality', that is, 'of living as a distinct and unique being among equals' (Arendt, 1971: 178, 247). Multiplicity also suggests that it is not just (certain) humans to whom things appear, and we wonder how others, including animals and plants, may appear as newcomers (in the sense of Arendt's natality), and how entrepreneurship may pluralistically enjoin these, as equals, into our midst. All this relates to entrepreneurship as a way of giving expression to the new and thereby settling it amidst the old and, for us at least, this speaks to a very exciting and open approach to theorising entrepreneurship. We were also struck by the ways in which phenomenology re-inserts the entrepreneur as a thinking, affective, perceiving being who has feelings and bodily sensations and how this can be a painful, unsettling and disturbing experience and as such it holds the potential for novelty arising from out of this uncanny sense of not quite belonging.

To us, this also makes entrepreneurship education different from only learning how to manage or administrate organisational affairs as it starts not with given resources and given aims, but it elicits these, together, and it is precisely through the process of creating such distinctions, being able to sense and hold on to dissonances and oddities, that the entrepreneur also emerges. In this sense, entrepreneurs may not need to be strong characters or equipped with specific traits or talents, but cultivate a sensitivity to the world they live in, exposing themselves to the strangeness of life and drawing inspiration from this unsettledness. Perhaps a difference to the artist, whose work can end with bringing the strange to an audience's attention, is that the entrepreneur turns strangeness into familiarity. This is where the hard slog of work comes in: budgets, prototypes, convincing others and all the myriad other things required to get an organisation off the ground. But it starts with a fleeting moment that requires cultivation to take on shape and form.

Holt (2018) speaks of this quality in the context of judgement as a concern for the pastoral. This is a 'play with dissonance' which emerges from one's attunement to how all things, however pretty or orderly or stable they appear, are really subject to a temporal span. The wilting, disintegrating, disorderly and deathly aspects are part of their finite existence. Entrepreneurship comes into its own when it stays clear of mindless repetition and of seeking comfort in habits, socially accepted norms and the numbing pleasantness of nostalgia and when it is alive to the frailty of human creation, its wondrous surprises and beguiling oddities as well as its arbitrary imbalances and exclusions, its grim injustices and its barbaric violence, meted out against fellow humans, animals and the natural world. Once we realise that this, all of this, could be different, we do not need to search for opportunities 'out there'. They are there in plentiful abundance, when we acknowledge that the world we see is just one of the many appearances it can have and that different ways of looking create, rather than just reflect, new ways of being. This ought to be unsettling but it also introduces a liberating, emancipatory and heretic 'punk' (Drakopoulou Dodd, 2014) element to entrepreneurship, which makes it a more profound and more important topic than the mere stimulation of economic enterprise. 'Teaching' entrepreneurship ought not be a one-way street but a dialogue between those already schooled in the ways of the world and the next generation of those entering it, bringing with them their own ideas and views. Can classrooms (but also cities, streets and other places) become sites in which plays of dissonance are acted out? Perhaps that is too tall an order for every single lecture or seminar, and there are many 'everyday' elements of starting and running a business that have to be included as well. But drawing on the many sources of more dissonant and more creative thinking, in literature, film, philosophy or the arts, combined with fostering spaces for caring and open dialogue among committed participants may go a long way to keep entrepreneurship special.

We have written about technology because it intervenes at all these levels: we notice through technologies and we make sense of things though them. We notice the world looking at excel sheets or the interfaces of customer management or business planning systems. We remember by using databases and videos stored in online clouds, but we remember also less directly when we are 'fed' information over interfaces or sensors, or when systems make decisions for us. However, we can never quite trace back what we notice or remember to anything that might have occurred; we are dealing with abstractions, analytical reductions and mediated artefacts instead. The growing influence of technology also makes interesting times for entrepreneurship where, as we have suggested, the notion of creativity looms large. We still have a tendency to cling on to the notion of the entrepreneur as the originator of creativity, understood as a human capacity, and we, too, have written about sensing and imagining, about folding coffee cups and inventing language. The next years will show how much such human interventions still matters next to the calculative immensity offered by connected computing systems, which can spew out novelty in unfiltered masses. Such advanced technologies are now an inextricable part of the entrepreneurial environment (McLuhan, 1964). We are still too familiar with our new, technologized world, as we were with the world of television and radio before, to put it into perspective. What ways of living and organising will emerge depends to a big part on how entrepreneurs notice the strangeness of this new world, and how they help organise life. Crucial in all this will be that entrepreneurs do not act against their worlds by extracting and violating their surroundings for temporary gain, but that they are part of the world they influence, making their flourishing dependent on the wellbeing of all our environment. Entrepreneurship cannot be disconnected from the question of what is a good life.

acknowledgements

We would like to thank Christina Lubinski, Daniel Hjorth and Robin Holt for commenting on drafts of this book. We are grateful to Jeni Zundel for contributing the drawing.

References

Adams, S. B. (2021) From orchards to chips: Silicon Valley's evolving entrepreneurial ecosystem. *Entrepreneurship & Regional Development*, 33 (1–2): 15–35.

Aichele, K.P. (2006) *Paul Klee, Poet/Painter*. Rochester, NY: Camden House.

Aldrich, H. E., & Ruef, M. (2018) Unicorns, Gazelles, and other distractions on the way to understanding real entrepreneurship in the United States. *Academy of Management Perspectives*, 32(4): 458–472.

Allen, T. (2007) A toy store(y)! *Journal of Business Venturing*, 22: 628–636.

Anders, G. (2016) On Promethean shame. In *Prometheanism*. Translated by C. J. Müller. London: Rowman & Littlefield. pp. 29–96.

Arendt, H. (1971) *The human condition*. Chicago: University of Chicago.

Arvidsson, A. (2020) Capitalism and the commons. *Theory, Culture & Society*, 37(2): 3–30.

Audretsch, D. (2015) *Everything in its place: Entrepreneurship and the strategic management of cities, Regions, and States*. Oxford: OUP.

Audretsch, D. B. (2021) Have we oversold the Silicon Valley model of entrepreneurship? *Small Business Economics*, 56(2): 849–856.

Augier, M. (2004, June) James march on education, leadership, and Don Quixote: Introduction and interview. *The Academy of Management Learning and Education*, 3(2): 169–177.

Baker, T., & Welter, F. (2024) Silicon Valley entrepreneurship-revisiting a popular dream. *Journal of Business Venturing Insights*, 21: 1–7.

Balabkins, N. W. (2006) Adaption without attribution? The genesis of Schumpeter's innovator. In J. G. Backhaus (ed). *Joseph Alois Schumpeter: Entrepreneurship, style and vision* (Vol. 1, pp. 203–220). Heidelberg: Springer Science & Business Media.

Balakrishnan, S. (2017) The Afropolitan idea: New perspectives on cosmopolitanism in African studies. *History Compass*, 15(2): 1–11.

Barbrook, R., & Cameron, A. (1996) The Californian ideology. *Science as Culture*, 6(1), 44–72.

Barbrook, R. (2015) (with A. Cameron). *The internet revolution: From dot-com capitalism to cybernetic communism*. Amsterdam: Colophon.

Bateson, G. (1979) *Mind and nature: A necessary unity*. New York: Dutton

Bateson, G. (1987) *Steps to an ecology of mind*. London: Jason Aronson.

Berglun, H., Bousfiha, M., & Mansoori, Y. (2020) Opportunities as artefacts and entrepreneurship as design. *Academy of Management Review*, 825–846.

Beyes, T., & Holt, R. (2020) The topographical imagination: Space and organization theory. *Organization Theory*, 1(2). https://doi.org/10.1177/2631787720913880

Beyes, T. (2015) Fictions of the possible: Art, the city and public entrepreneurship. *Journal of Management Inquiry*, 24: 445–449.

Blank, S., & Dorf, B. (2012) *The startup owner's manual: The step-by-step guide for building a great company*. Pescadero: K&S Ranch.

Blank, S., & Dorf, B. (2020) *The startup owner's manual: The step-by-step guide for building a great company*. John Wiley & Sons.

Blank, S. (2012) Why the lean start-up changes everything. *Harvard Business Review*.

Boje, D. (2016) Critique of the triple bottom line. In G. A. Rosile (ed) *Tribal wisdom for business ethics* (pp. 181–198). London: Emerald.

Burton, T. I. (2023) Rational magic. *The New Atlantis*, Spring 2023, 72: 3–17.

Casper, S. (2007) *Creating Silicon Valley in Europe: Public policy towards new technology industries*. Oxford: Oxford University Press.

Certeau, M. (1988) *The practice of everyday life*. Berkley: University of California.

Chesbrough, H., & Rosenbloom, R. S. (2002) The role of the business model in capturing value from innovation: Evidence from Xerox Corporation's technology spin-off companies. *Industrial and Corporate Change*, 11(3): 529–555.

Chia, R., & Holt, R. (2009) *Strategy without design: the silent efficacy of indirect action*. Cambridge: Cambridge University Press.

Clarke, J. S., Cornelissen, J. P., & Healey, M. P. (2019) Actions speak louder than words: How figurative language and gesturing in entrepreneurial pitches influences investment judgments. *Academy of Management Journal*, 62(2): 335–360.

Cooper, M. (2021) The Alt-Right: Neoliberalism, libertarianism and the fascist temptation. *Theory, Culture & Society*, 38(6): 29–50.

Dart, R. (2018) Bursting the bubble: The mythologies of many social enterprises and enterpri $ ing nonprofits. In P. Dey & C. Steyaert (eds.) *Social entrepreneurship* (pp. 65–72). Cheltenham: Edward Elgar Publishing.

Davis, W., & Gane, N. (2021) Post-Neoliberalism? An introduction. *Theory, Culture & Society*, 38-6: 3–28.

Dey, P., & Mason, C. (2018) Overcoming constraints of collective imagination: An inquiry into activist entrepreneuring, disruptive truth-telling and the creation of 'possible worlds'. *Journal of Business Venturing*, 33(1): 84–99.

Dey, P., & Steyaert, C. (2018) *Social entrepreneurship: an affirmative critique*. Cheltenham: Elgar.

Didion, J. (2021) *Let me tell you what I mean*. New York: Knopf.

Dimov, D., Schaefer, R., & Pistrui, J. (2021) Look who is talking ... and who is listening: Finding an integrative "we" voice in entrepreneurial scholarship. *Entrepreneurship Theory and Practice*, 45(5): 1176–1196.

Dimov, D. (2011) Grappling with the unbearable elusiveness of entrepreneurial opportunities. *Entrepreneurship Theory and Practice*, 35(1): 57–81.

Dimov, D. (2020) Opportunities, language, and time. *Academy of Management Perspectives*, 34(3): 333–351.

Drakopoulou Dodd, S. D., & Anderson, A. R. (2007) Mumpsimus and the mything of the individualistic entrepreneur. *International Small Business Journal*, 25(4): 341–360.

Drakopoulou Dodd, S. L. D. (2014) Roots radical–place, power and practice in punk entrepreneurship. *Entrepreneurship & Regional Development*, 26(1–2): 165–205.

Doherty, B., Haugh, H., & Lyon, F. (2014) Social enterprises as hybrid organizations: A review and research agenda. *International Journal of Management Reviews*, 16(4): 417–436.

Doody, S. (2020) Reactionary technopolitics: A critical sociohistorical review. *Fast Capitalism*, 17(1): 143–163.

Doolin, B. (2002) Enterprise discourse, professional identity and the organizational control of hospital clinicians Bill Doolin. *Organization Studies*, 23(3): 369–390.

Drucker, P. (1985) *Entrepreneurship and innovation: Practice and principles*. New York: Harper Business.

Drucker, P. (2015) *Innovation and entrepreneurship: Practice and principles*. London, Routledge.

Ehrenzweig, A. (1971) *The hidden order of art*. Berkeley: University of California Press.

Ehrig, T., & Foss, N. J. (2022) Why we need normative theories of entrepreneurial learning that go beyond Bayesianism. *Journal of Business Venturing Insights*, 18: e00335.

Farrow, R. (2023) Elon Musk's shadow rule. *The New Yorker*. https://www.newyorker.com/magazine/2023/08/28/elon-musks-shadow-rule

Fisher, M. (2009) *Capitalist realism*. Washington: Zero Books.

Fisher, M. (2018) *k-punk: The collected and unpublished writings of Mark Fisher (2004–2016)*. Edited by Darren Ambrose. Repeater.

Florida, R. (2002) *The rise of the creative class*. New York: Basic Books.

Galison, P. (1994, Autumn) The ontology of the enemy: Norbert Wiener and the cybernetic vision critical inquiry, 21(1): 228–266.

Gartner, W. B. (1988) Who is the entrepreneur? Is the wrong question. *American Journal of Small Business*, 11–32.

Gersel, J., & Thaning, M. S. (2022) Some philosophical help with "neoliberalism". In D. S. Souleles, J. Gersel, & M. S. Thaning (eds.) *People before markets: An alternative casebook* (pp. 10–53). Cambridge: Cambridge University Press.

Grey, C. (2005) *A very short, fairly interesting and reasonably cheap book about studying organizations*. London: SAGE.

Groz, E. (2008) *Chaos, territory, art: Deleuze and the framing of the earth*. New York: Columbia.

Hall, J. K., Daneke, G. A., & Lenox, M. J. (2010) Sustainable development and entrepreneurship: Past contributions and future directions. *Journal of Business Venturing*, 25(5): 439–448.

Hardt, M., & Negri, A. (2017) *Assembly*. New York: Oxford University Press.

Hepp, A., Schmitz, A., & Schneider, N. (2023) Afterlives of the Californian ideology| afterlives of the Californian ideology: Tech movements, pioneer communities, and imaginaries of digital futures—Introduction. *International Journal of Communication*, 17: 19.

Hernan, L, & Ramirez-Figueroa, C. (2021) Domesticity and digital eugenics: Design cultures of Silicon valley. In *Cumulus Conference Proceedings Roma 2021*. Track: Design Culture (of) THINKING, pp. 4542–4550.

Hietschold, N., Voegtlin, C., Scherer, A. G., & Gehman, J. (2023) Pathways to social value and social change: An integrative review of the social entrepreneurship literature. *International Journal of Management Reviews*, 25: 564–586.

Hjorth, D., & Holt, R. (2016) Nietzsche as an educator. In C. Steyaert, T. Beyes, & M. Parker (eds.) *The Routledge companion to reinventing management education* (pp. 107–119). London: Routledge.

Hjorth, D., & Holt, R. (2016) It's entrepreneurship, not enterprise: Ai Weiwei as entrepreneur. *Journal of Business Venturing Insights*, 5: 50–54.

Hjorth, D., & Johannisson, B. (2008) Building new roads for entrepreneurship research to travel by: On the work of William B. Gartner. *Small Business Economics*, 31: 341–350

Hjorth, D., & Steyaert, C. (2021) Stirring and disturb-urging the movement of academic entrepreneurship onwards. In P. Eriksson, H. Hytti, K. Komulainen, T. Montonen & P. Siivonen (Eds.), *New movements in academic entrepreneurship* (pp. 254–268). Cheltenham: Edward Elgar Publishing.

Hjorth, D., Holt, R. & Styeaert, C. (2015) Entrepreneurship and process studies. *International Small Business Journal*, 33(6): 599–611.

Hjorth, D. (2004) Creating space for play/Invention – Concepts of space and organizational entrepreneurship. *Entrepreneurship & Regional Development*, 16: 413–432.

Hjorth, D. (2007) Lessons from Iago: Narrating the event of entrepreneurship. *Journal of Business Venturing*, 22(5): 712–732.

Hjorth, D (2014) Sketching a philosophy of entrepreneurship. In Baker, T., & Welter, F. (eds.) *The Routledge companion to entrepreneurship* (pp. 41–58). London: Routledge.

Holm, D. V., & Beyes, T. (2022) How art becomes organization: Reimagining aesthetics, sites and politics of entrepreneurship. *Organization Studies*, 43(2): 227–245.

Holt, R. (2018) *Judgment and strategy*. Oxford: OUP.

Imas, J. M., Wilson, N., & Weston, A. (2012) Barefoot entrepreneurs. *Organization*, 19(5): 563–585.

Ingold, T. (2011) *Being alive: Essays on movement, knowledge and description*. London: Routledge.

Johnsen, C. G., Olaison, L., & Sørensen, B. M. (2018) Put your style at stake: A new use of sustainable entrepreneurship. *Organization Studies*, 39(2–3): 397–415.

Jones, W. (2006) *Grayson Perry: Portrait of the artist as a young girl*. London: CHATTO & WINDUS.

Jullien, F. (2004) *In praise of blandness: Proceeding from Chinese thought and aesthetics*. New York: Zone Books.

Juma, C. (2016) *Innovation and its enemies: why people resist new technologies* (1st ed.). New York: Oxford University Press.

Kirzner, I. M. (1997) Entrepreneurial discovery and the competitive market process: An Austrian approach. *Journal of Economic Literature*, 35(1): 60–85.

Kirzner, I. M. (2009) The alert and creative entrepreneur: A clarification. *Small Business Economics*, 32(2): 145–152.

Klee, P. (1956) *Notebooks, Vol. 1: The thinking eye*. London: Lund Humphries.

Klein, J. (2009) *Grayson Perry*. London: Thames & Hudson.

Knight, F. H. (1921) *Risk, uncertainty and profit*. New York: Cosimo Classics.

Kociatkiewicz, J., Kostera, M. (2020) Defense of the comfort zone: Against the hegemony of creative destruction. In Örtenblad, A. (eds) *Against entrepreneurship* (pp. 203–223). Cham: Palgrave Macmillan.

Kohn, E. (2013) *How forests think: Toward an anthropology beyond the human.* Berkeley: California University Press.

Kurzweil, R. (2005) *The singularity is near: When humans transcend biology.* New York: Viking Press.

Law, J. (2004) *After method: Mess in social science research.* London: Routledge.

Lilley, S., & Lightfoot, G. (2014) The embodiment of neoliberalism: Exploring the roots and limits of the calculation of arbitrage in the entrepreneurial function. *The Sociological Review*, 62(1): 68–89.

Mair, J., & Marti, I. (2009) Entrepreneurship in and around institutional voids: A case study from Bangladesh, *Journal of Business Venturing*, 24(5): 419–435.

Mair, J., & Martí, I. (2009) Entrepreneurship in and around institutional voids: A case study from Bangladesh. *Journal of Business Venturing*, 24: 419

Manjoo, F. (2022) What is happening to the people falling for crypto and nfts. *The New York Times.* https://www.nytimes.com/2022/05/05/opinion/crypto-nfts-web3.html

Martinez Dy, A., Jayawarna, D., & Marlow, S. (2024) Racial capitalism and entrepreneurship: An intersectional feminist labour market perspective on UK self-employment. *Sociology.* March 16, 2024.

Massumi, B. (2002) *Parables of the virtual: Movement, affect, sensation.* London: Duke.

Mbebe, A. (2020) Afropolitanism. *Journal of Contemporary African Art.* 46(May): 56–62.

Mbebe, A. (2021) *Out of the dark night.* New York: Columbia University Press.

McCloskey, D., & Mingardi, A. (2020) *The myth of the entrepreneurial state.* Great Barrington: AIER.

McCloskey, D. (2006) *The bourgeois virtues: Ethics for an age of commerce.* Chicago: University of Chicago Press.

McCraw, T. (2007) *Prophet of innovation: Joseph Schumpeter and creative destruction.* Cambridge: Belknap.

McLuhan, M. (1964) *Understanding Media: The extensions of man.* Berkeley: Ginko Press.

McNay, L. (2009) Self as enterprise: Dilemmas of control and resistance in Foucault's the birth of biopolitics. *Theory, Culture & Society*, 26(6): 55–77.

Merleau-Ponty, M. (1964/1993) *The primacy of perception.* ed. James M. Edie, trans. Carleton Dallery, Evanston: Northwestern University Press, 1964. Revised by Michael Smith in The Merleau-Ponty Aesthetics Reader, Galen A. Johnson, ed. Evanston: Northwestern University Press.

Mirowski, P. (2002) *Machine dreams: Economics becomes a cyborg science.* Cambridge: Cambridge University Press.

Morgan, M. (2012) *The world in the model how economists work and think.* Cambridge: Cambridge University Press.

Morozov, E. (2013) *To save everything, click here: The folly of technological solutionism.* New York: PublicAffairs.

Muñoz, P., & Cohen, B. (2018) Sustainable entrepreneurship research: Taking stock and looking ahead. *Business Strategy and the Environment,* 27(3): 300–322.

Munro, R. (2018) Creativity, organization and entrepreneurship: Power and play in the ecological process of money. *Organization Studies,* 9(2–3): 209–227.

Nietzsche, F. (1996) *Human, all too human.* Trasl. R. J. Hollingdale. Cambridge: Cambridge University Press.

Olaison, L., & Sørensen, B. (2014) The abject of entrepreneurship: Failure, fiasco, fraud. *International Journal of Entrepreneurial Behavior & Research,* 20(2): 193–211.

Penrose, E. (1995) *The theory of the growth of the firm.* Oxford. Oxford University Press.

Perry, G. (2015) *Playing to the gallery: Helping contemporary art in its struggle to be understood.* London: Penguin Books.

Peukert, H. (2006) The missing chapter in Schumpeter's the theory of economic development. In J. G. Backhaus (ed.), *Joseph Alois Schumpeter: Entrepreneurship, style and vision* (Vol. 1, pp. 221–232). Boston: Springer Science & Business Media.

Pickering, A. (2010) *The cybernetic brain.* Chicago: University of Chicago Press.

Plehwe, D. (2020) Schumpeter revival? How neoliberals revised the image of the entrepreneur. In D. Phlewe, Q. Slobodian, & P. Mirowski (eds.) *Nine lives of neoliberalism* (pp. 120–142). London and New York: Verso.

Popp, A., & Holt, R. (2013) The presence of entrepreneurial opportunity. *Business History,* 55(1): 9–21.

Ramoglou, S., & McMullen, J. S. (2024) 'What is an opportunity?': From theoretical mystification to everyday understanding. *Academy of Management Review,* 49(2): 273–298.

Reckwitz, R. (2017) *The invention of creativity.* Cambridge: Polity.

Reinert, H., & Reinert, E. S. (2006a) Creative destruction in economics: Nietzsche, Sombart, schumpeter. Friedrich Nietzsche (1844–1900). *Economy and Society*, 55–85.

Reinert, H., & Reinert, E. S. (2006b) Creative destruction in economics: Nietzsche, Sombart, Schumpeter. In J. G. Backhaus, & W. Drechsler (eds.), *Friedrich Nietzsche (1844–1900). The European heritage in economics and the social sciences* (vol 3, pp. 55–85). Boston: Springer.

Ries, E. (2011) *The lean startup*. New York: Crown Business. 27, 2016–2020.

Rindova, V., Barry, D., & Ketchen, D. J. (2009) Entrepreneuring as emancipation. *Academy of Management Review*, 34(3): 477–491.

Rorty, R. (1989) *Contingency, irony, and solidarity*. New York: Cambridge University Press.

Safranski, R. (2002) *Nietzsche: a philosophical biography*. Trasl. Shelley Frish. London: Granta.

Sarasvathy, S. (2001) Causation and effectuation: Toward a theoretical shift from economic inevitability to entrepreneurial contingency. *Academy of Management Review*, 28(20: 243–263.

Schuetz, A. (1951) Choosing among projects of action. *Philosophy and Phenomenological Research*, 12(2): 161.

Schumpeter, J., Becker, M. C., & Knudsen, T. (2002) Theorie der wirtschaftlichen Entwicklung. *The American Journal of Economics and Sociology*, 61(2): 405–437.

Schumpeter, J. A. (1934) *The theory of economic development*. Cambridge: Harvard University Press.

Schumpeter, J. (1942/2003) *Capitalism, socialism and democracy*. London: Routledge.

Schumpeter, J. A. (1947) The creative response in economic history. *The Journal of Economic History*, 7(2): 149–159.

Schumpeter, J. (1947) The creative response in economic theory. *The Journal of Economic History*, 7(2): 149–159.

Schumpeter, J. (2002/1911) Theorie der wirtschaftlichen Entwicklung. Translated by Markus C. Becker and Thorbjørn Knudsen. *The American Journal of Economics and Sociology*, 61(2): 405–437.

Schumpeter, J. A. (2003) *Capitalism, socialism and democracy*. London: Routledge.

Scott, J. C. (1998) *Seeing like a state: How certain schemes to improve the human condition have failed*. New Haven: Yale.

Shane, S., & Venkataraman, S. (2000) The promise of entrepreneurship as a field of research. *Academy of Management Review*, 25(1): 217–226.

Simon, H. (1996) *The sciences of the artificial*. Cambridge, MA: MIT.

Simondon, G. (2012) Technical mentality (Transl. A. de Boever). In A. de Boever, A. Murray, J. Roffe, & A. Wood (eds.), *Gilbert Simondon: Being and technology*. Edinburgh: Edinburgh University Press.

Smith, R., & McElwee, G. (2014) Informal, illegal and criminal entrepreneurship. In T. Baker, & F. Welter (eds.), *The Routledge companion to entrepreneurship* (pp. 244–261). London: Routledge.

Smith Hughes, S. (2009) *Dennis, Reid. 2009. Early Bay Area Venture Capitalists: Shaping the Economic and Business Landscape*. An oral history conducted by Sally Smith Hughes in 2009, Regional Oral History Office, The Bancroft Library. Berkeley: University of California. https://digitalassets.lib.berkeley.edu/roho/ucb/text/dennis _reid.pdf. Accessed 2020.

Something Ventured interview. Interview by Dayna Goldfine. *Libraries. Department of Special Collections and University Archives*. Stanford University. https://purl.stanford.edu/wx351zf0148. Accessed 2020.

Sørensen, B. M. (2008) 'Behold, I am making all things new': The entrepreneur as savior in the age of creativity. *Scandinavian Journal of Management*, 24(2): 85–93.

Spinosa, C., Dreyfus, R.,& Flores, F. (1997) *Disclosing new worlds: Entrepreneurship, democratic action, and the cultivation of solidarity*. Cambridge: MIT.

Staff, C. (2017) A poetics of becoming: The mythgraphy of Cy Twombly. In: J. Hirsh (ed.), *Contemporary art and classical myth* (pp. 43–52) London: Routledge.

Steyaert, C. (2007) Of course that is not the whole (toy) story: Entrepreneurship and the cat's cradle. *Journal of Business Venturing*, 22(5): 733–751.

Steyaert, C. (2014) Going all the way: The creativity of entrepreneuring in the Full Monty. In C. Bilton, & S. Cummings (eds), *Handbook of management and creativity* (pp. 160–182). Cheltenham and Northampton: Edward Elgar Publishing.

Teasdale, S., Lyon, F., & Owen, R. (2018) A methodological critique of the social enterprise growth myth. In P. Dey, & C. Steyaert (eds.), *Social entrepreneurship* (pp. 19–39). Cheltenham: Edward Elgar Publishing.

Temkin, A. (1987) *Klee and the Avant-Garde*. Edited by C. Lancher. Paul Klee. Boston: Little, Brown & Co., pp. 13–39.

Thiel, P. (2014) *Zero to one: Notes on startups, or how to build the future*. New York: Crown.

Tilley, C. (2004) *The materiality of stone explorations in landscape phenomenology: 1*. Oxford: Berg.

Tsoukas, H., & Chia, R. (2002) On organizational becoming: Rethinking organizational *Change Organization Science*, 13(5): 567–582

Turner, F. (2006) *From counterculture to cyberculture – Stewart Brand, the whole earth network, and the rise of digital utopianism*. Chicago: University of Chicago Press.

University of Cambridge Judge Business School (2024) *Cambridge Centre for Alternative finance*. https://ccaf.io/cbeci/index

Von Foerster, H. (2003) *Understanding: Essays on cybernetics and cognition*. New York: Springer.

Wadhwani, R. D., & Lubinski, C. (2017) Reinventing entrepreneurial history. *Business History Review*, 91(4): 767–799.

Welter, F., Baker, T., Audretsch, D. B., & Gartner, W. B. (2017) Everyday entrepreneurship—A call for entrepreneurship research to embrace entrepreneurial diversity. *Entrepreneurship Theory and Practice*, 41(3): 311–321.

Welter, F., Baker, T., Audretsch, T., & Gartner, B. (2017) Everyday entrepreneurship: A call for entrepreneurship research to embrace entrepreneurial diversity. *Entrepreneurship, Theory and Practice*, May, 311–322.

Wiedeman, R. (2020) *Billion dollar loser: The epic rise and spectacular fall of Adam Neumann and WeWork*. New York: Little, Brown.

Wilson, E. (2018) *Homer: The Odyssey. Transl. E. Wilson*. New York: Norton.

Woods, C., Dell, K., & Carroll, B. (2022) Decolonizing the business school: Reconstructing the entrepreneurship classroom through indigenizing pedagogy and learning. *The Academy of Management Learning and Education*, 21(1): 82–100.

Yang, M. (2023) The vast majority of NFTs are now worthless, new report shows. *The Guardian*. https://www.theguardian.com/technology/2023/sep/22/nfts-worthless-price

Zuboff, S. (2019) *The age of surveillance capitalism: The fight for a human future at the new frontier of power*. PublicAffairs.

Zundel, M. (2012) Walking to learn: rethinking reflection for management learning. *Management Learning*, 44(2): 109–126.

Index